Messages From God

....

Devotions for Everyday Trials

Vince Jackson

Copyright © 2024 by Vince Jackson

All rights reserved.

No part of this publication may be reproduced, distributed, or transmitted in any form or by any means, including photocopying, recording, or other electronic or mechanical methods, without the prior written permission of the publisher, except in the case of brief quotations embodied in critical reviews and certain other noncommercial uses permitted by copyright law.

Dedication

This book is dedicated to my mom, Eunice Jackson Webb. Thank you for your love and guidance. I am blessed to have had you.

~Vince

TABLE OF CONTENTS

Dedication iii
The Favor of God 1
The Power Of Thankfulness 5
Praise Before Your Breakthrough 9
God Is Enough So Be Thankful 16
The Power Of Thankfulness 20
Brag On God, Brag about God 24
Our Forgetfulness and Lack Of Appreciation 32
Have A Continuing Moving Forward Perspective 39
Adjusting Your Perspective 44
Your Persistent Perspective Determines Your Presence 49
Trust God 53
Why Should We Love God? 57
Having Humility 61
God Is In Control 65
Stop Sharing Gossip and Spread the Gospel 70
This Little Light Of Mine I'm Going To Let It Shine 76
Loving God Requires Us To Focus On The Things Of God 82
To Grow In God's Love Requires Soul Alignment 86
Sometimes We Have To Pushing Our Way Past Our Pain 92
Your Focus Is Required to Love 97
What Season Are You In? 101
Learn to Forgive And Let Go To Heal 106
Letting Go To Gain 110
Everything Has A Season 116

Our Forgiveness Allows Us to Find God 120
Emotions Are Not Your Enemy But Neither Should They Be Your Guide 124
It Belongs To God 129
Fleeing From Temptation 133
The Hardships of Being Favored 139
Learning How To Let It Go 143
Attitude Of Gratefulness 147
Learning To Forgive 151
Wanting To Be Better 155
God's Wisdom vs The World Schemes 159
The Gift of Generosity 164
Do You Have What You Need? 169
Let Your Trials Make You More Like Jesus 173
God Honors Me 179
God Answers My Call 184
I Am Seated With Him On High 187
God Is My Deliverer 191
We Do Not Have To Fear Destruction 196
We Do Not Have To Fear The Pandemic or Other Pestilence 200
I Will Not Fear The Arrow 204
The Protection of God 209
The Shield Of God 215
Protection Under His Wings 218
My Deliverance 222
Dwelling Place In My Secret Place 226

Drawing Near to God 232
Learn To Abide in the Love of God... 236
Increasing Love for God.. 240
His Angels Shall Watch Over Me 244
Though A Thousand Fall 248
About the Author 253
References 255

The Favor of God

Many of us assume that we lack God's favor because we sometimes deal with a lot of foolishness, but I'm here to tell you today that sometimes we go through a lot of foolishness because we have found favor with God. Joseph was taken by his brothers and sold into slavery, landing in prison because he had favor. David was chased by his father-in-law, who tried to kill him because he found favor. Esther was placed in an uncomfortable position because she found favor. Favor doesn't mean that life will be easy because, to be honest, when you find favor with God, you will face challenges from Satan and people.

So, what is Favor with God?

It's knowing that, regardless of the situation you are in, God will protect, deliver, and bless you. It's a divine kindness, or an act of true compassion on the part of God Himself toward our needs and, sometimes, undeserving lives as His people.

There is nothing like the favor of God. God's favor opens doors that no man can shut and shuts doors no man can open. It brings prosperity and breakthroughs, especially when people try to harm and hurt us.

God's favor can radically change your circumstances and your position. Having God's favor on your life is one of the most powerful things that can be released to you. Matthew 6:33 says, "Seek ye first the kingdom of God, and his righteousness, and all these things shall be added unto you.

SCRIPTURE REFERENCES

Isaiah 58:11
The LORD will guide you always; he will satisfy your needs in a sun-scorched land and will strengthen your frame. You will be like a well-watered garden, like a spring whose waters never fail.

Ephesians 1:11
In him we were also chosen,

having been predestined according to the plan of him who works out everything in conformity with the purpose of his will,

Psalms 30:5
For his anger lasts only a moment, but his favor lasts a lifetime; weeping may stay for the night, but rejoicing comes in the morning.

Psalms 90:17
May the favor of the Lord our God rest on us; establish the work of our hands for us— yes, establish the work of our hands.

Proverbs 3:33-35

33 The LORD's curse is on the house of the wicked, but he blesses the home of the righteous.

34 He mocks proud mockers but shows favor to the humble and oppressed.

35 The wise inherit honor, but fools get only shame.

2

The Power Of Thankfulness

Psalm 100:1-5

Make a joyful noise unto the Lord, all ye lands.

2 Serve the Lord with gladness: come before his presence with singing.

3 Know ye that the Lord he is God: it is he that hath made us, and not we ourselves; we are his people, and the sheep of his pasture.

4 Enter into his gates with thanksgiving, and into his courts with praise: be thankful unto him, and bless his name.

5 For the Lord is good; his mercy is everlasting; and his truth endureth to all generations.

King David was likely the greatest worship leader of all time. He understood how powerful being thankful was to his success as a believer in Christ and how it helped him overcome numerous challenges in life. Consider this for a moment: when Samuel came to his father looking for the next king among his sons, his father didn't even think highly enough of him to bring him into the house to meet with the other brothers. When he inquired about why nobody wanted to fight Goliath, his brother told him to shut up. Furthermore, his father-in-law not only tried to kill him, but also took his wife and gave her to another man!

Now, that would be enough for most of us to shut down, give up, and complain to God or even blame God for all that we were going through. However, David knew God, and he understood that in Psalm 30:5:" For his anger endureth but a moment; in his favour is life: weeping may endure for a night, but joy cometh in the morning."

See, I just believe that David knew that what he was going through didn't define who he was or what he was experiencing. I believe that David was trusting God to be the same God who helped him defeat the wild animals threatening his flock, the same God who gave him victory over Goliath, and the same God who protected him when his father-in-law and his army were chasing him, attempting to kill him. David believed that God was even the same God who delivered him when he messed up. He knew that Jesus died for his sins, giving him many reasons to be thankful.

When we enter into our prayers with thankfulness, just before we start asking for things or complaining about them, there are so many things that will be revealed to our understanding. Thankfulness positions our hearts for greater awareness and openness to God.

REFERENCES SCRIPTURES

James 1:3-6
3Knowing this, that the trying of your faith worketh patience.

4 But let patience have her perfect work, that ye may be perfect and entire, wanting nothing. 5 any of you lack wisdom, let him ask of God, that giveth to all men liberally, and up braideth not; and it shall be given him.

6 But let him ask in faith, nothing wavering. For he that wavereth is like a wave of the sea driven with the wind and tossed.

_____

_____

_____

_____

_____

_____

_____

_____

_____

_____

_____

_____

_____

_____

_____

_____

_____

_____

_____

_____

Praise Before Your Breakthrough

If you truly want to be delivered, blessed, protected and loved, learn to praise God before your breakthrough, and if you really want to make Satan mad and defeated just believe God in your praise and claim it.

The Hebrew words of praise is "Hallel." Unrestrained, David danced and praised the Lord in ecstatic delight as he watched the Ark of the Lord being brought back to Jerusalem. The Bible tells us in 2 Samuel 6 that all of Israel rejoiced with shouts and the sound of trumpets. There are a number of them, and each of them have such a profound meaning and implication for the way we worship. One of the words, towdah, is a type of expressive praise that typically implies giving thanks to God for things "not yet received."

God wants us to show our extended faithfulness and trust in Him even in the midst of challenges and difficulties and our praise is required and it's power.

The power of our praise connects us with God, it inhabits or enthrones us as his people. When you magnify God through your praise, worship and singing of His wonderous works—from creation to the cross and into eternity—we invite Him into our lives and sometimes we can't wait until Sunday. Sometimes I go out on my deck and God and I have church. I sing, I cry, and I praise him for keeping me when I was a fool out there in the world. I praise God for what he's doing in my life, and I praise and thank Him for what he is going to do in my life.

In the Book of Daniel the 6th Chapter

Daniel praised God no matter what was going on or who told him not to because he understood that praising God has a greater power than anything that man thinks he has control over.

Scripture Reference s

Daniel 6:

1 It pleased Darius to set over the kingdom an hundred and twenty princes, which should be over the whole kingdom;

2 And over these three presidents; of whom Daniel was first: that the princes might give accounts unto them, and the king should have no damage.

3 Then this Daniel was preferred above the presidents and princes, because an excellent spirit was in him; and the king thought to set him over the whole realm.

4 Then the presidents and princes sought to find occasion against Daniel concerning the kingdom; but they could find none occasion nor

fault; forasmuch as he was faithful, neither was there any error or fault found in him.

5 Then said these men, We shall not find any occasion against this Daniel, except we find it against him concerning the law of his God.

6 Then these presidents and princes assembled together to the king, and said thus unto him, King Darius, live forever.

7 All the presidents of the kingdom, the governors, and the princes, the counsellors, and the captains, have consulted together to establish a royal statute, and to make a firm decree, that whosoever shall ask a petition of any God or man for thirty days, save of thee, O king, he shall be cast into the den of lions.

8 Now, O king, establish the decree, and sign the writing, that it be not changed, according to the law of the Medes and Persians, which altereth not.

9 Wherefore king Darius signed the writing and the decree.

10 Now when Daniel knew that the writing was signed, he went into his house; and his windows being open in his chamber toward Jerusalem, he kneeled upon his knees three times a day, and prayed, and gave thanks before his God, as he did aforetime.

11 Then these men assembled, and found Daniel praying and making supplication before his God.

12 Then they came near, and spake before the king concerning the king's decree; Hast thou not signed a decree, that every man that shall

ask a petition of any God or man within thirty days, save of thee, O king, shall be cast into the den of lions? The king answered and said, The thing is true, according to the law of the Medes and Persians, which altereth not.

13 Then answered they and said before the king, That Daniel, which is of the children of the captivity of Judah, regardeth not thee, O king, nor the decree that thou hast signed, but maketh his petition three times a day.

14 Then the king, when he heard these words, was sore displeased with himself, and set his heart on Daniel to deliver him: and he laboured till the going down of the sun to deliver him.

15 Then these men assembled unto the king, and said unto the king, Know, O king, that the law of the Medes and Persians is, That no decree nor statute which the king establisheth may be changed.

16 Then the king commanded, and they brought Daniel, and cast him into the den of lions. Now the king spake and said unto Daniel, Thy God whom thou servest continually, he will deliver thee.

17 And a stone was brought, and laid upon the mouth of the den; and the king sealed it with his own signet, and with the signet of his lords; that the purpose might not be changed concerning Daniel.

18 Then the king went to his palace, and passed the night fasting: neither were instruments of musick brought before him: and his sleep went from him.

19 Then the king arose very early in the morning, and went in haste unto the den of lions.

20 And when he came to the den, he cried with a lamentable voice unto Daniel: and the king spake and said to Daniel, O Daniel, servant of the living God, is thy God, whom thou servest continually, able to deliver thee from the lions?

21 Then said Daniel unto the king, O king, live for ever.

22 My God hath sent his angel, and hath shut the lions' mouths, that they have not hurt me: forasmuch as before him innocency was found in me; and also before thee, O king, have I done no hurt.

23 Then was the king exceedingly glad for him, and commanded that they should take Daniel up out of the den. So Daniel was taken up out of the den, and no manner of hurt was found upon him, because he believed in his God.

24 And the king commanded, and they brought those men which had accused Daniel, and they cast them into the den of lions, them, their children, and their wives; and the lions had the mastery of them, and brake all their bones in pieces or ever they came at the bottom of the den.

25 Then king Darius wrote unto all people, nations, and languages, that dwell in all the earth; Peace be multiplied unto you.

26 I make a decree, That in every dominion of my kingdom men tremble and fear before the God of Daniel: for he is the living God,

and stedfast for ever, and his kingdom that which shall not be destroyed, and his dominion shall be even unto the end.

27 He delivereth and rescueth, and he worketh signs and wonders in heaven and in earth, who hath delivered Daniel from the power of the lions.

28 So this Daniel prospered in the reign of Darius, and in the reign of Cyrus the Persian.

Not only is our praise required it's also protected, it's honors and please God.

When we can give thanks before we see our breakthrough. The power of your praise will determine the magnitude of your breakthrough. Praise is not just clapping your hands or applauding God. It is showing respect, honor, and gratefulness using your whole heart, mind, spirit and body despite your circumstances.

Now this is powerful your breakthrough is your praise, I need somebody to know that I need somebody to praise him right now, your breakthrough has already happened he's just waiting on your praise.

_____
_____
_____
_____
_____
_____

4

GOD IS ENOUGH SO BE THANKFUL

Matthew 14-21

14 And Jesus went forth, and saw a great multitude, and was moved with compassion toward them, and he healed their sick.

15 And when it was evening, his disciples came to him, saying, This is a desert place, and the time is now past; send the multitude away, that they may go into the villages, and buy themselves victuals.

16 But Jesus said unto them, They need not depart; give ye them to eat.

17 And they say unto him, We have here but five loaves, and two fishes.

18 He said, Bring them hither to me.

19 And he commanded the multitude to sit down on the grass, and took the five loaves, and the two fishes, and looking up to heaven, he blessed, and brake, and gave the loaves to his disciples, and the disciples to the multitude.

20 And they did all eat, and were filled: and they took up of the fragments that remained twelve baskets full.

21 And they that had eaten were about five thousand men, beside women and children.

I've read this story over and over several times, and it really is quite an amazing story, but I need someone to understand the miracle wasn't that the bread and fish was enough the miracle happened because Jesus prayed a prayer of being thankful.

Before Jesus passed out the bread and fish, He first gave thanks for it. He gave thanks to God for what he was going to do. He didn't complain to God about not having enough. I'm often reminded about how Job had more than enough but rather than being thankful he often prayed a prayer of fear and later on after all his earthly treasures were gone, he prayed a prayer of complaining. It wasn't until Job shut up long enough to listen to God that he realized what things God had done in his life and what he was going to do in his life that he realized that he still had many things to be thankful for too many of us Believers are walking around right now complaining about what we don't have and are not being thankful for what God is doing in our lives.

I need you to think about if you have ever been caught up in what you lack that you can't be thankful for what you gained? How many times has God kept you when you were walking around out there acting a fool and he protected you? How many times where you wondering how you were going to pay a bill, and he made a way?

We can get so preoccupied with what we don't have that we don't have any gratitude for what we do have.

God tells us in 1 Thessalonians 5:18

in everything give thanks; for this is the will of God in Christ Jesus for you.

When we are thankful God will use our gratitude to bless us with even more. When we look for things to be thankful for, it brings peace and joy to our lives, and it opens up our hearts understanding along with our eyes so that we can use the light in the tunnel. We don't have to wait until we get to the end of the tunnel, start thanking and praising Him in the tunnel.

SCRIPTURE REFERENCE

Matthew 25:23

His lord said unto him, 'Well done, good and faithful servant. Thou hast been faithful over a few things; I will make thee ruler over many things. Enter thou into the joy of thy lord.

_____
_____
_____
_____
_____
_____

5

THE POWER OF THANKFULNESS

Psalm 100:1-5

Make a joyful noise unto the Lord, all ye lands.

2 Serve the Lord with gladness: come before his presence with singing.

3 Know ye that the Lord he is God: it is he that hath made us, and not we ourselves; we are his people, and the sheep of his pasture.

4 Enter into his gates with thanksgiving, and into his courts with praise: be thankful unto him, and bless his name.

5 For the Lord is good; his mercy is everlasting; and his truth endureth to all generations.

King David was probably the greatest worship leader of all time. He understood just how powerful being thankful was to his success as a Believer in Christ and how he was able to overcome so many challenges in life. Think about it for a second: when Samuel came to his father looking for the next king among his sons, his daddy didn't even think enough of him to bring him in the house to meet with the other brothers. When he inquired about why nobody wanted to fight Goliath, his brother told him to shut up, his father in law not only tried to kill him but also took his wife from him and gave her to another man! Now that would be enough for most of us to shut down, give up and complain to God or even blame God for all that we were going through, but David knew God and he knew that in Psalm 30:5

For his anger endureth but a moment; in his favour is life: weeping may endure for a night, but joy cometh in the morning.

See I just believe that as David endured so much more, he knew that what he was going through didn't define who he was or what he was going through. I believe that David was trusting God to be the same God that helped him defeat the wild animals from killing his flock, the same God that gave him victory over Goliath, the same God that protected him when his father in-law and his army was chasing him trying to kill him that he was even the same God that delivered him even when he messed up. See David knew who God was therefore there so were many reasons to be thankful. When we enter into our prayers being thankful you know just before we start asking for stuff or complaining about stuff, if we will enter our prayers with thankfulness then there so many things that will be revealed to our understanding.

Thankfulness positions our hearts for greater awareness and openness to God.

SCRIPTURE REFERENCE

James 1:3-6
3Knowing this, that the trying of your faith worketh patience.

4But let patience have her perfect work, that ye may be perfect and entire, wanting nothing. 5 any of you lack wisdom, let him ask of God, that giveth to all men liberally, and upbraideth not; and it shall be given him.

6 But let him ask in faith, nothing wavering. For he that wavereth is like a wave of the sea driven with the wind and tossed.

_____
_____
_____
_____
_____
_____
_____
_____
_____
_____
_____
_____
_____
_____
_____
_____
_____

6

BRAG ON GOD, BRAG ABOUT GOD

Now if any of you guys truly know me then you know that I'm not short of confidence and you know I will never need anyone else to toot my horn. I'm good at doing for myself. Now oftentimes people don't understand I have a purpose with this: one it empowers me to feed off of myself and the second reason, I'm confident in how God made me. Let me tell you this, the only one that is totally worth of being lifted up is God, and not only is he worthy of my praise, but he's worthy of me bragging about his goodness.

When we brag on God, He loves to show up and show out. When we tell people about all the amazing things He's done or doing in our lives it gives Him permission to do it again.

In 2nd Chronicles 5, Solomon is dedicating the newly built temple to God. And the worship leaders begin to lead the people in giving thanks to God, singing "Give thanks to the Lord, for He is good. His love endures forever."

Over and over and over they begin to thank God and praise Him, and what happens next is amazing. It says that the glory of God came and filled the temple; so much so that the priests literally couldn't keep going; they all just stood in awe.

When we begin to praise God it sets us free physically, mentally, emotionally and spiritually to be delivered, protected, prepared and to receive his love and blessings.

In our praise, in our worship, God is building YOU as a temple, and wants to fill you in the same way.

Our boasting on God cause other Believers to admire him as much as we admire him. We are seeking praise—for Christ's worth.

Boasting in the Lord - in him builds our faith and that of other believers It reminds us of our heritage in God, how much He loves us and His infinite capabilities.

1 Corinthians 1:31—"Therefore, as it is written, 'Let him who boasts boast in the Lord.'"

May I never boast except in the cross of our Lord Jesus Christ, through which the world has been crucified to me, and I to the world" (Galatians 6:14).

Jeremiah 9:23

Thus says the Lord, "Let not a wise man boast of his wisdom, and let not the mighty man boast of his might, let not a rich man boast of his riches;

1 Corinthians 1:31

so that, just as it is written, "Let him who boasts, boast in the Lord."

2 Corinthians 10:17

But he who boasts is to boast in the Lord.

Psalm 34:2

My soul will make its boast in the Lord;

The humble will hear it and rejoice.

Psalm 44:8

In God we have boasted all day long,

And we will give thanks to Your name forever. Selah.

Psalm 20:7

Some boast in chariots and some in horses,

But we will boast in the name of the Lord, our God. Being Thankful

Why is it so important for a Believer to be thankful? Gratitude helps us see God's hand is all over our circumstances. When we give God our thanks it opens up our hearts to receive more of his blessings and more of his grace. It gives us a peace that surpasses all understanding.

When we have a gratitude of thanksgiving it increases our awareness of God and give us clears connection to Him.

In positive psychological research, gratitude is strongly and consistently associated with greater happiness. Gratitude helps people feel more positive emotions, relish good experiences, improve their health, deal with adversity, and build strong relationships.

Philippians 4:6-7 - "Do not be anxious about anything, but in every situation, by prayer and petition, with thanksgiving, present your requests to God.

1 Thessalonians 5:16-18. Rejoice always, pray continually, give thanks in all circumstances; for this is God's will for you in Christ Jesus.

Psalm 107:1

Oh give thanks to the Lord, for he is good, for his steadfast love endures forever!

Now I could go on and on with scriptures on why I should be thankful but let me see if I can bring clarity and educate us all on the powerful anointing that takes place in our lives when we have the Spirit of Gratitude. When we are thankful it takes away from us focusing on negative things and situations. When we are thankful, we are also being hopeful. When we learn to be thankful we are expecting God to fix our situation because we realize ALL the stuff that He protected us through when we were not fit to live but weren't ready to die, when we were fools out there in the world and didn't know if we were coming or going, see I know sometimes the way gets difficult but I'm thankful right now because I know that no weapon formed against me shall prosper. I'm thankful that I know weeping endures for a night, but joy comes in the morning. I'm thankful because I know my God prepare me a table in the mist of my enemies and Vince is going to eat no matter what the enemy tries to do. Guys I found out that my brother Cliff is serious about the eating part so don't y'all try and come between him and God especially during that time, you are looking for problems!

Too many times we focus on what we don't have but what someone else has, sometimes we have to be thankful and happy when God blesses someone else instead of being jealous especially if we know they represent God. Be honest would you want to be reading messages from someone that aren't never got their stuff together, always being ungrateful or do you want to celebrate with a winner, because guys I can tell you for certainty all I do is win. See I've actually read the end of the book you know where the archangel Michael defeated Satan. I'm one of God's soldiers and I know that I have to put on the full armor of God each day. If David would have had his armor on and doing what God had told him he wouldn't have gone through his foolishness. There were a lot of reasons that Job went through what he had to go through. He had a lot of stuff but it was stuff that he was afraid of losing instead of stuff that he was grateful for.

I truly believe that Gratefulness is just as powerful Spiritual Anointing as Love, Faith, Trust, and Obedience

One of the most convicting passages in scripture is in Romans 1. In it, Paul talks about how all of nature itself is proof of the existence of God. That God's qualities are "clearly seen" because of creation, and therefore, men are "without excuse."

So, sounds like God's existence should be pretty clear to everyone, right? You'd think. But something happened to dampen or cut off mankind's awareness to God. That made what should be so easily seen, hidden. Paul says that though they knew Him, they did not honor Him or "give Him thanks," and as a result, their "foolish hearts were darkened."

In case you missed it, I'll spell it out. When we don't give thanks, our hearts are darkened and the connection to God that we were made for grows fuzzy. Thanksgiving is the hinge. It's small and unassuming, yet with it, a door is able to swing wide open, but a door without hinges isn't a door; it's a wall.

We need thanksgiving. We need that hinge that opens wide the door of our hearts to God. Maybe you've been feeling disconnected from God. Like your connection is off. Like what once was so clear now seems foggy.

I've got an idea for you. Start thanking Him.

Use that hinge. In the same way that when we don't thank God, our connection grows dim, when we do thank Him, things begin to become clear again.

Thanksgiving opens our awareness to God. Thank Him.

SCRIPTURE REFERENCE

Romans 1:18-23.

Think about where your heart has grown dark in your awareness of God. Repent for ways you've turned away from Him, and start giving Him thanks. Find a place where you can do it out loud; there is power to the spoken word. God didn't think "let there be light!" He spoke it! Give thanks to the Lord. Put on a praise song that speaks of gratitude for what He's done. Make this a regular practice in your life, and I believe that your awareness of God will grow.

7

OUR FORGETFULNESS AND LACK OF APPRECIATION

It has been said that man's first mistake wasn't disobedience, it was forgetfulness and lack of appreciation for what God had done in their lives.

Let's go back to the beginning

Book of Genesis 1: 26-28

26 And God said, Let us make man in our image, after our likeness: and let them have dominion over the fish of the sea, and over the fowl of the air, and over the cattle, and over all the earth, and over every creeping thing that creepeth upon the earth.

27 So God created man in his own image, in the image of God created he him; male and female created he them.

28 And God blessed them, and God said unto them, Be fruitful, and multiply, and replenish the earth, and subdue it: and have dominion

over the fish of the sea, and over the fowl of the air, and over every living thing that moveth upon the earth.

Genesis 2 :15-25

15 And the Lord God took the man, and put him into the garden of Eden to dress it and to keep it.

16 And the Lord God commanded the man, saying, Of every tree of the garden thou mayest freely eat:

17 But of the tree of the knowledge of good and evil, thou shalt not eat of it: for in the day that thou eatest thereof thou shalt surely die.

18 And the Lord God said, It is not good that the man should be alone; I will make him an help meet for him.

19 And out of the ground the Lord God formed every beast of the field, and every fowl of the air; and brought them unto Adam to see what he would call them: and whatsoever Adam called every living creature, that was the name thereof.

20 And Adam gave names to all cattle, and to the fowl of the air, and to every beast of the field; but for Adam there was not found an help meet for him.

21 And the Lord God caused a deep sleep to fall upon Adam, and he slept: and he took one of his ribs, and closed up the flesh instead thereof;

22 And the rib, which the Lord God had taken from man, made he a woman, and brought her unto the man.

23 And Adam said, This is now bone of my bones, and flesh of my flesh: she shall be called Woman, because she was taken out of Man.

24 Therefore shall a man leave his father and his mother, and shall cleave unto his wife: and they shall be one flesh.

25 And they were both naked, the man and his wife, and were not ashamed.

Now let's think about this for a second. This was a perfect union between God, man, and woman but somehow in spite of all the things that God had made available to them they allowed the snake (you know that person at church that stays in everybody business, that person at work that tries to make the job harder) to come in and break it up. He was able to do that because they didn't keep their minds on God and somewhere in all of that they forgot they were already like God didn't he say that they were created in his image and seemingly they didn't appreciate all that he was doing in their lives. They lacked nothing but was looking for something that they already had. When we start looking away from God we will allow Satan to make us forget all that God is doing, has done in our lives and we stop appreciating all that he's kept us through, knowing we haven't been what we are supposed to be but he kept us, I understand better now when the old Saints would say, "Ain't fit to live but ain't ready to die." Most of us still praying about what we don't have instead of having a thankful prayer about what we do have, we walk around complaining about what we ain't got and can't appreciate what we do have. Let's go to one of my favorite Books of the Bible.

Scripture Reference

Psalms 23 23 The Lord is my shepherd; I shall not want.(He's our provider)

2 He maketh me to lie down in green pastures: he leadeth me beside the still waters.(I have food and water)

3 He restoreth my soul: he leadeth me in the paths of righteousness for his name's sake. (He's my guide)

4 Yea, though I walk through the valley of the shadow of death, I will fear no evil: for thou art with me; thy rod and thy staff they comfort me. (He's my protector)

5 Thou preparest a table before me in the presence of mine enemies: thou anointest my head with oil; my cup runneth over. (He's my preparer)

6 Surely goodness and mercy shall follow me all the days of my life: and I will dwell in the house of the Lord for ever. (He gives me prosperity and I have a place in heaven waiting for me)

Now tell who don't want to serve a God like this?

Now I often get mad at Adam and Eve when I especially on Monday mornings when I have to go back to work but God will convict me and tell me, you know that you also have your moments when you have forgotten or haven't appreciated all that I've done for you, protect you from or provided for you.

See we all have those same moments that Adam and Eve had we forget or don't appreciate his goodness and his kindness for us.

We forget God's goodness. We forget His nature. We forget how faithful He's been, and the promises and provision He has for us.

King David knew this. In Psalm 103, He says "Bless the Lord my soul, and forget not His benefits".

Forget not the things He has done. Forget not His goodness. Forget not how time after time He does amazing things. And David doesn't just leave it abstract and intangible. He then goes on and lists the things God has done. He counts his blessings to remind himself of who God is.

And of you know this song

Count Your Blessings, Johnson Oatman Jr.

Lyrics

1. When upon life's billows you are tempest-tossed, When you are discouraged, thinking all is lost, Count your many blessings; name them one by one, And it will surprise you what the Lord has done.

[Chorus]Count your blessings; Name them one by one. Count your blessings; See what God hath done. Count your blessings; Name them one by one. Count your many blessings; See what God hath done.

2. Are you ever burdened with a load of care? Does the cross seem heavy you are called to bear? Count your many blessings; every doubt will fly, And you will be singing as the days go by.

3. When you look at others with their lands and gold, Think that Christ has promised you his wealth untold. Count your many blessings; money cannot buy Your reward in heaven nor your home on high.

4. So amid the conflict, whether great or small, Do not be discouraged; God is over all. Count your many blessings; angels will attend, Help and comfort give you to your journey's end.

_____
_____
_____
_____
_____
_____
_____
_____
_____
_____
_____
_____
_____
_____
_____
_____
_____
_____

HAVE A CONTINUING MOVING FORWARD PERSPECTIVE

Isaiah 43:19 NLT says, "For I am about to do something new. See, I have already begun! Do you not see it? I will make a pathway through the wilderness. I will create rivers in the dry wasteland."

Too many times we allow our past to keep us from moving forward and it has a negative impact on our perspective, outlook, progress, and relationships with God.

One of the worst things you can do in a race is to look behind you because just as sure as you do people will pass you because you are focused on their progress and not yours. I also learned that in basketball if someone is beating you down court then you must put your head down so that you don't watch them dribbling because you will start moving at the pace of the ball and they will beat you. Now let's apply these concepts into our lives as Believers. If we are constantly worrying about what happened yesterday: who hurt you, who talked about you, what you didn't get, then it's impossible for you to move forward on your journey. I need you to know this trail that you are on it's about you and God not you and Sam. Now what business is it of yours if God has chosen to bless someone else. We can't see our blessings or move where God wants to bless us because instead of being happy for Sam, we're mad at him and God because apparently he's making more progress on his trail then we are because he's trusting God and ain't looking at you.

Psalms 121:1 will lift up my eyes to the hills— From whence comes my help? I'm focused on what God what's from me and for me not what someone else has or doing.

And let me add this I don't care what you have been through or going through God is God and there's nothing more powerful, more loving, and more capable than him.

Now I understand that we all have dealt with something addictions, low self-esteem, depression, lying, loneliness, and I know that in rehabs it's important to acknowledge those things, but I also know that you are not that person anymore when you become a Believer. You can leave those things behind, but you have to empty your pockets because God has something better for you to put in them.

SCRIPTURE REFERENCE

2 Corinthians 5 :6-17

6Therefore we are always confident, knowing that, whilst we are at home in the body, we are absent from the Lord:

7 (For we walk by faith, not by sight:)

8 We are confident, I say, and willing rather to be absent from the body, and to be present with the Lord.

9 Wherefore we labour, that, whether present or absent, we may be accepted of him.

10 For we must all appear before the judgment seat of Christ; that every one may receive the things done in his body, according to that he hath done, whether it be good or bad.

11 Knowing therefore the terror of the Lord, we persuade men; but we are made manifest unto God; and I trust also are made manifest in your consciences.

12 For we commend not ourselves again unto you, but give you occasion to glory on our behalf, that ye may have somewhat to answer them which glory in appearance, and not in heart.

13 For whether we be beside ourselves, it is to God: or whether we be sober, it is for your cause.

14 For the love of Christ constraineth us; because we thus judge, that if one died for all, then were all dead:

15 And that he died for all, that they which live should not henceforth live unto themselves, but unto him which died for them, and rose again.

16 Wherefore henceforth know we no man after the flesh: yea, though we have known Christ after the flesh, yet now henceforth know we him no more.

17 Therefore if any man be in Christ, he is a new creature: old things are passed away; behold, all things are become new

Behold, I will do a new thing; now it shall spring forth; shall ye not know it? I will even make a way in the wilderness, and rivers in the desert."

Isaiah 43:19 KJV

Fear thou not; for I am with thee: be not dismayed; for I am thy God: I will strengthen thee; yea, I will help thee; yea, I will uphold thee with the right hand of my righteousness.

Isaiah 41:10 KJV

Be careful for nothing; but in every thing by prayer and supplication with thanksgiving let your requests be made known unto God.

Philippians 4:6 KJV

Take therefore no thought for the morrow: for the morrow shall take thought for the things of itself. Sufficient unto the day is the evil thereof.

Matthew 6:34 KJV

Set your affection on things above, not on things on the earth.

_____
_____
_____
_____
_____
_____

9

ADJUSTING YOUR PERSPECTIVE

Listen I know it can difficult at times, and we all seem to be waiting to get to the light at the end of the tunnel. I can't tell you how many times friends have tried to encourage me with that phrase or how many times I've used it to try and encourage someone else, but I have some really good news for you from God. Why are we waiting to get to the end of the tunnel to see the light when he has given you the light so that you don't stumble on your journey to him? We keep thinking we won't get blessed, delivered, or overcome situations, beat addictions, overcome financial problems and etc. until we get to the end of the tunnel to the light, when the purpose of the light is to keep us from stumbling on our journey. The light is not the blessings, you are, and the things that you learn about God and yourself while in the darkness. When we learn to be blessed, to be delivered, to be saved during the darkest when we get to the light, it's there we realize it was God that guided our path on our journey.

Matthew 6:22 NLT says, "Your eye is like a lamp that provides light for your body. When your eye is healthy, your whole body is filled with light."

KJV 22 The light of the body is the eye: if therefore thine eye be single, thy whole body shall be full of light.

See the light is not at the end of the tunnel. You are the light so no matter where you are or what you are going through, as long as you keep your eyes on God you will get there.

Now I understand scientifically speaking, human vision is unable to distinguish anything without illumination. How can our eyes act as a lamp in a dark situation?

Because we continue to look into the physical body instead of approaching our situation in the spiritual. Your Fight, Your Deliverance, and Your Victory is not Physical. It's A Spiritual War!

Light at the end of the tunnel. The first thing I will challenge you to do is shift your perspective of the "light at the end of the tunnel." It's easy to view the light as simply an escape or exit from dark times. We exclaim, "If I can only make it to that light, I will be out of here!" The issue with that simplistic view is it does not allow room for "life." Some days we feel like we make significant progress, but most days we trip, stumble, and sometimes fall as we focus on the exit and not the things around us. That makes the light seem like a distant dream or "hope deferred."

Psalms 119:105 KJV says, "Thy word is a lamp unto my feet, And a light unto my path."

When we learn to use the light as our resource and not our source we begin to learn and grow from the dark environment. We recognize and quickly step over stumbling blocks in your path that you previously would have missed, you know the things that Satan put there to trip us up. At first God will show us how to move around them, but the more we understand that God is our light, we learn to use those very stumbling blocks underneath our feet. God will make our enemies our footstool.

SCRIPTURE REFERENCE

Romans 8:28 NLT. Be comforted in the fact that your path will become brighter and brighter as you traverse dark times. You can and will make it! I believe in you!

KJV 28 And we know that all things work together for good to them that love God, to them who are the called according to his purpose.

Jeremiah 29:11

For I know the thoughts that I think toward you, saith the LORD, thoughts of peace, and not of evil, to give you an expected end."

1 Peter 5:10

But the God of all grace, who hath called us unto his eternal glory by Christ Jesus, after that ye have suffered a while, make you perfect, stablish, strengthen, settle you."

Ecclesiastes 3:11,14

He hath made every thing beautiful in his time: also he hath set the world in their heart, so that no man can find out the work that God maketh from the beginning to the end. I know that, whatsoever God doeth, it shall be for ever: nothing can be put to it, nor any thing taken from it: and God doeth it, that men should fear before him.

Your Persistent Perspective Determines Your Presence

What does it mean to be persistent?

Firm or obstinate continuance in a course of action in spite of difficulty or opposition.

Now what is perspective?

A particular attitude toward or way of regarding something; a point of view.

Because of what Jesus did on the cross for us, he endured the cross not only to save us but also to encourage us not to grow weary and lose heart. Troubles abound in this sin-wracked world, but God says we're blessed when we persevere under trials (James 1:12). In order to endure, we must rid ourselves of sin and obstacles and maintain a positive, persistent, perspective of what God is doing in our lives.

Now I truly believe we learn life's lessons in so many places in my weight room, it's full of things that can either crush you or make you stronger. It all depends on your perspective. When you are lifting its tearing your muscles down, but when you are persistent and continue its building muscle and strength, and your perspective changes for something more positive and you want more of it and you are willing to seek it more, but here's the thing, the more you do it the easier it becomes to achieve your goals.

Why is perspective important for Christians?

It is an exhortation to think according to faith and Scripture. This Christian teaching is that our minds, our ways of thinking, and our perspectives are not to be merely points of view, responses, and reactions to things based upon our feelings, or our preferences. It is a discipline to be undertaken.

One day I noticed one of my brothers was a little down because he was struggling with something. Now I want ALL of you to know that's also not uncommon for a Believer but I also know that you don't have to go through this by yourself. Not only will God provide for you but I'm here and there's also some very good people in this group with you that has been there and we don't judge we love and support one another so don't make the excuse "I'm dealing with this by myself" and there's also a brother that I need each of you to keep in your prayers.

Sometimes as Believers we must adjust the PERSPECTIVE of our THOUGHTS!

I remember there were three guys that I worked out with and if you know me I'm very competitive. Well I was the smallest in weight, but I could out lift them all except on bicep day. I mean every time it came to the preacher curl bar I would complain and have a negative perspective about doing biceps, but one of the guys said "Vince if you change your perspective you can change your outcome." So at first I was playing with it, but on bicep day I started speaking positive and yes I started out-lifting them in that area also.

Now there's been times in my life that hasn't been easy and at first when I ministered I preached a lot of sermons on making it through until one day God spoke to me and said, "Vince you have made it through so I need you to tell someone else they have made it, they just have to change their perspective and expect it so they will see all the positives that will continue to get better."

Scripture Reference

Luke 18:1-8 tells of a widow who was not receiving justice for her case, so she continued to pester the judge and would not take "no" for an answer. Because the widow persisted in her pleas for justice, the ungodly judge finally relented and gave her what she asked. Jesus then challenged His followers to persist in their prayers the same way.

_____
_____
_____
_____
_____
_____
_____
_____

11

TRUST GOD

Now I know that's easier said than done, sometimes especially when we are dealing with foolishness, grief, depression, and sometimes the things that seem to make us happy that God will not approve of.

When Lord is speaking to us, we can trust He's always telling us the right things to do. Today, let's place our full dependence on Him, knowing His character and guidance are worthy of our trust.

Why is it important for Christians to trust God?

God knows everything we are going through, everything that we will go through, and now here's the most important part: He will not allow you to go through anything by yourself and He's only going to allow you to go through what will strengthen you, educate you, and prepare you. Each situation that we face he has gone before you and prepared the way and even fixed some of the situations where we created the problems. I'm reminded of how Jacob deceived his brother and had to flee and then after deceiving his uncle he had to run right back to his brother, but he was afraid because of what he did to his brother but I loved what Jacob did the night before meeting his brother as he prayed he wouldn't be turned loose from God until he could hear God's voice and his instructions. Sometimes we have to toil over our situations until God gives us instructions to move, some of us leave a church because someone pissed us off, but God didn't say move. We will leave a job that God has every intention of blessings us on but because someone is giving us a hard time instead of praying to God we leave. I don't care what it looks like or who says, I don't even care if your entire family and the family dog is mad at you do what God has told you to do but I also need you to trust him enough to approach each situation knowing that you can trust God completely and that he is going to work it out. There are so many times on my job that we are faced with something that's difficult, and they will come to me for answers, or someone will say that it's going to be impossible to do and I'll start praying and God will show me how to accomplish the impossible. They have that "we cannot spy" mentality, but I have a Joshua mentality. God has given us the victory but if we don't move on it, we will never see it or experience his greatness.

To trust is to believe in the reliability, truth, ability, or strength of what God is doing.

When it comes to trusting God, that means believing in His reliability, His Word, His ability, and His strength. The Bible says that God cannot lie. That He always keeps His promises. That He loves you and has good in store for you.

SCRIPTURE REFERENCE

Proverbs 3:5-7 says, "Trust in the Lord with all your heart; do not depend on your own understanding. Seek His will in all you do, and He will show you which path to take. Do not be impressed with your own wisdom. Instead, fear the Lord and turn away from evil."

Why Should We Love God?

Yes, I know that most of us were raised to believe the Bible and to love God, but again my question is, why? Because we are made in his image and made for him by him.

In Genesis 1:26 says, "Then God said, 'Let Us make man in Our image, according to Our likeness...'" Not only were we created in our Creator's image, but we were also created to enjoy intimacy and fellowship with Him. In fact, He is the only reason for our existence.

So why does he allow us to go through so much at times? Because he knows difficult times teaches us life lessons the same as good times and it brings spiritual growth and lessons that we need to defeat Satan. I think of it like when I do basketball training or weight training, I work more on the things that's difficult for my players because I'm preparing them for battle. I weight train them so they can endure the physicality of the game. The reason God allows us to go through some of our difficult times is because he knows the trying of our faith is more precious than gold and he knows that our faith needs to be strong for this fight that we are in and Believers make no mistake about it we are in a fight! The good news is that Satan knows it too, but he wants to make it as hard as possible for you but the more we trust God, the more we surrender it to God, the more we learn about God and the more we stay in his presence the easier our battle becomes because we become battle tested. Most people assume I coach basketball simply because of the love for the game which I do love it but more importantly I love the relationships that I've built with these young athletes, and I know each game we are in a battle. There's no in-between when I show up in a gym. They either love me or in most cases they hate me. All I do is win and I'm not talking about the score, but I do that too but I have a opportunity to win lives for God and Satan is mad as hell that he can't stop that or the score.

Now don't get me wrong sometimes I do fall short but I believe those are the times that I need to grow because sometimes we can allow circumstances to alter or change about how we feel about or how much we want to trust God but I think those are the times when need to search ourselves and remember all the things that he's delivered you from.

What we think about His goodness and His power.

When things are going well, we can think He's great. When life gets tough, we can start believing He doesn't care about us.

Scripture Reference

In Hebrews 13:8 confirms that "Jesus Christ is the same yesterday and today and forever." So he hasn't changed he died for us so do you really think he's left you to deal with things on your own, he left the Holy

Spirit here to guide, protect and shield you the problem is something we move away from that protection physically and mentally.

Psalm 18:30 says, "This God—His way is perfect; the Word of the Lord proves true; He is a shield for all those who take refuge in Him."

Isaiah 40:28 declares, "Have you not known? Have you not heard? The Lord is the everlasting God, the Creator of the ends of the earth. He does not faint or grow weary; His understanding is unsearchable."

_____
_____
_____
_____
_____
_____
_____
_____
_____
_____
_____
_____
_____
_____
_____
_____
_____
_____

13

HAVING HUMILITY

What is humility? A modest view of one's own importance for something better.

Why is it important in the lives of Believers? Humility allows us to fully submit to God - God wants us to acknowledge that apart from Him we can do nothing. He is the one who knows us, the one who created us.

Jalen Hurts has become one of the top quarterbacks in the NFL and he's a really good example of what humility is. This guy lost his starting quarterback job on national television, but instead of blaming everyone or letting it destroy him, he used it to lift up God and God used it to elevate him. He even stayed at the University of Alabama for another year and came off the bench to help them win the SEC Championship. He knew that God had something better for him and he also knew that he couldn't move until God told him to move. Sometimes we move away from problems before we allow God to fix those problems, and sometimes we move because we are more concerned with what people think or say about us. Now I don't say this grudgingly but I wish that I had stayed a little longer at the church were the Pastor discussed by business with someone else because I don't run from I've learned to walk to places that God has placed me because I know that he has a reason but we have to be humble enough to know it's not about us, but it's about why God has you were you are and doing what God has called you to do.

There are two aspects of this incredible story that should encourage us as Believers. First how Jalen stayed humble in the sideline encouraging his teammates, and his ability to stay positive when they interviewed him.

In Matthew 23:12: "Whoever exalts himself shall be humbled, and whoever humbles himself shall be raised to honor."

Sometimes we don't know how our ability to handle trying situations affects other Believers and what examples we set.

Humility is so important because God makes it clear in His Word that He, because of His lowliness and His humility, is repulsed by pride, and pride separates us from God as we do not acknowledge and appreciate the eternal sovereignty of our Lord.

In Hebrews 11:1&40

1. Now faith is the substance of things hoped for, the evidence of things not seen.

40. God having provided some better thing for us, that they without us should not be made perfect. I believe that as a Believer in Christ you also need that I believe, I trust and that I'm going to ride with God even if the wheels fall off.

I work for a company that can really make me mad at times and I've been trying to quit for 40 years now and there's so many things that I have to do to make things work around there and sometimes I don't feel appreciated by them. I also know everything that I have accomplished there is due to a direct obedience of listening to God. One day I was complaining so much that it was almost like God hit me over the head when he asked me why are you complaining instead of praying. Guys sometimes we think we praying when we are actually complaining, you know it wasn't until Job stopped complaining and stop thinking it's about him that God healed him and God told me that it ain't about me but my brother Cliff and my children, Kelvin, Chris, Lump, Emma, Travis, Terri, William, Tracy, Tony and a lot more that God has placed in my life which I've been richly blessed to have a relationship with.

So sometimes we just need to shut up, be humble and be about God's business and he will take care of yours.

Scripture Reference

Matthew 23:12

"And whosoever shall exalt himself shall be abased; and he that shall humble himself shall be exalted."

God Is In Control

When we learn that God really is in control, and that he always wins we should be able to give him full trust, full surrender, and our full attention. To be honest there's very little that we can control because if you ask Val or Sabrina they will tell you that Cali controls me and you know what I had the same effect on my pawpaw.

I think the biggest problem we have as Believers is that we continue to fight a spiritual war trying to use physical tools.

Ephesians 6:12
For we are not fighting against flesh-and-blood enemies, but against evil rulers and authorities of the unseen world, against mighty powers in this dark world, and against evil spirits in the heavenly places.

When we can accept this reality, it can either lead us to a place of despair, or a true surrender to God. Part of realizing that so much is out of our control is the acceptance that everything is in God's control and that his is worthy to be trusted.

Despite living in a sin accepted world today God is still in control, let me add this because apparently some of us Believers haven't read how this war that we are in ends.

Revelation 12:7-10

Michael and his angels fought against the dragon, and the dragon and his angels fought back. 8 But he was not strong enough, and they lost their place in heaven. 9 The great dragon was hurled down—that ancient serpent called the devil, or Satan, who leads the whole world astray.

He is God, and we are not. Since life is not up to us, this should lead to peace. Worry and fear take over when we think we're in charge, but the sooner we admit we're not, the better off we'll be.

Romans 11:33-36 declares, "Oh, how great are God's riches and wisdom and knowledge! How impossible it is for us to understand His decisions and His ways! For who can know the Lord's thoughts? Who knows enough to give Him advice? And who has given Him so much that He needs to pay it back? For everything comes from Him and exists by His power and is intended for His glory. All glory to Him forever! Amen."

The archangel's victory over the devil is won Michael is shown in violent motion, wings spread and flaming sword held aloft, standing over the devil. The vanquished devil, his face distorted with fear and horror, is tumbling head-first into the flames. Look I don't know about y'all but I've been on God's team for a long time and all we do is win, no matter what!

Let me add this and see if I can bring understanding. I'm a very good basketball trainer, I'm anointed to do it and although I thought Val was my best student, I'm learning that actually my grand boy is now. If you watch him practice you can't tell and sometimes you can't tell at the beginning of a game but let me tell you this, when the situation gets hot and it looks like the odds are impossible to overcome here comes Corey Lamar White Jr. AKA Doobie, my grandson. He get's down, so I trust him with the ball. Guys I can tell you for sure trouble will come but I'm telling you the ball in God's hand and watch him work. Here's the thing, you can't put it in his hand and you try and hold on to it also. Just throw the ball in and guard your man, on second thought if you get beat on a play God will pick up your slack but we have to first give him complete control and then we have to trust him with that control.

Scripture Reference

Psalm 135:6

The Lord does whatever pleases Him throughout all heaven and earth, and on the seas and in their depths. God is in control and knows what's best, so let's find peace as we believe this to be true. Let's also control what we can control and make decisions that honor God in the present.

Romans 11:33-34

O the depth of the riches both of the wisdom and knowledge of God! how unsearchable are his judgments, and his ways past finding out! For who hath known the mind of the Lord? or who hath been his counsellor? For of him, and through him, and to him, are all things: to whom be glory for ever. Amen.

Psalm 135:6

Whatsoever the LORD pleased, that did he in heaven, and in earth, In the seas, and all deep places.

Stop Sharing Gossip and Spread the Gospel

Too many Believers are quicker to share gossip, but not spread God's word, and it's sinful. The content of sinful gossip is never neutral.

We will share what we consider to be juicy information about someone even if we aren't sure if it's true and don't care about if it hurts them. Well, I have news for you-it's hurting your relationship with God. Sharing bad information—lies—about someone behind their back is sinful gossip.

The Lord promises us that "a false witness will not go unpunished, and he who pours out lies will not go free" (Prov. 19:5).

Most of the time here's what I've learned about people that always have something to tell you about someone else's business: they are waiting for your reaction or what you have to say so they can take it back and they have more skeletons in their closet than the person they are gossiping about.

Yes I know some of us think that if something is true, then it's not gossip. Not so. Gossip is also foolishly spreading that awful truth about someone. Proverbs tells us that "a gossip betrays a confidence, but a trustworthy man keeps a secret" (11:13). The secrets revealed by gossip are often the skeletons in someone's closet that do not really need to get out.

A biblical phrase for this is "a bad report" (Hebrew dibbah). Proverbs says, "Whoever spreads slander [dibbah] is a fool" (10:18).

Gossip hurts the whole body of Christ, when it's acceptable in your life, it hinders you from what important the word of God. It's because of gossip that so many churches are failing apart but let me say this also that still doesn't excuse you from not going to church, they gossip at work you still go.

I remember there was this man that started going to our church when I was still in high school and a couple of the women would talk about how tight he wore his pants, and before you knew it, it got back to him and he left the church. Later he became a very positive figure in God's house, and he was invited back to the church to preach and he talked about how gossip can hurt the church. Instead of talking about people, talk to people and you will find out ways to lift them up while lifting up Gods word, found out that the reason he worn those pants, he had fallen on hard times, and he knew that he needed to be in church and out of the streets but they almost ran him back into the streets. Thank God instead of going to the streets he went where Gods word was being taught and not people being talked about.

Gossips hurt neighbors, divide friends, and damage reputations and relationships. The Bible labels gossips as untrustworthy and meddlesome (Proverbs 11:13; 20:19; 26:20; 1 Timothy 5:13) — and even as worthy of death (Romans 1:29, 32).

If you're in a conversation with someone and it begins to move towards gossip about someone else, be willing to stop the conversation and name it for what it really is. "This is gossip. God is not honored by gossip. Gossip is a sin and God hates it. Malicious talk or gossip is mentioned elsewhere in the Bible, listed along with sins like murder and envy (Romans 1:29), things that should not be practiced or approved (verse 32). Proverbs 25:23, the verse that specifically uses the word backbiting, paints a vivid picture of how people respond to a gossip.

Believers Stop Gossiping!

Now that I've given it to you through scriptures let's talk about why gossiping does more to hurt the body of Christ than helping you to grow In Christ.

What is gossiping?

Being a part of a conversation about someone else private life usually listening to something that embarrassing about someone else's life but here's a few things that I've found out about people that bring you gossip, they are the same people that either gossip about your business or they take back what you said to that person and yes I believe it's a bigger problem in God's house than anywhere else. Now the Bible tells us why it's a sin but let go a little farther and see why it's so destructive.

1. It's sinful we have learned that

2. It's idolatrous, it can become your God(anything that you allow to replace God)

3. It's self-centered, we are focused on helping but judging

4. It's divisive, the quickest way to separate believers

5. It destroys trust, as a Pastor I was trusted with what other people were going through and there's no way that I was going to discuss their problems with anyone else except God, my Pastor apparently discussed something that I was going through with someone that he thought he could trust and before you know it most people in the church heard about it but when it got to them I was the one that was wrong but honestly I was the one being wronged so you can imagine what that did to our relationship

6. It's a stumbling block for others. (it keeps you and others from growing in unity and your relationship with God.

7. It's addictive, you can't get enough of it to satisfy you so you forget everything else just to get to it.

But we can resist gossip, we must recognize it. That's not as easy to do as it may sound. It is not always easy to recognize the moment when our "small talk" becomes sinful talk. In fact, if you're like me, then you regularly ask yourself during conversations, "Should I be saying this?" or, "Should I be listening to this?"

The hardest part about recognizing gossip is that it does not come with a warning label. There we are, just talking with someone, and seemingly out of nowhere this juicy piece of news about someone else presents itself and asks us to swallow it. And yes we should turn away from it but like all sin we just want to listen just a little and that just a little will have you completely messed up.

Now with my mom, you couldn't bring her gossip about anyone else business especially after church service because if you did she would take you directly to the person that you are talking about and tell them that you guys have a problem that you need to work out so you can imagine not a lot of people talked to her after service so I've adopted that same way. Now I understand that it's allowed in the church but it's not allowed in God's house.

Scripture Reference

Provers 21:23 KJV

"Whoso keepeth his mouth and his tongue Keepeth his soul from troubles."

_____
_____
_____
_____
_____
_____

16

THIS LITTLE LIGHT OF MINE I'M GOING TO LET IT SHINE

More than ever before way to many individuals are seeking the spotlight of personal glory in God's house, no I'm not talking about the building but I'm talking about their service to God.

Christians are called to shine brightly for the glory of God not to bring attention to themselves but to lift God up but now we have so many of them trying to shine their light by man for man and we can't figure out why Johnny has been going to 1st Anointed Of Christ Church all his life and he hasn't grown spiritually, don't know how to get a prayer through and don't have a personal relationship with God, but he get to tithe and sit up front every Sunday.

Let me see if I can explain why it's important to be in the service of God. Notice I didn't say go to church because there's a lot of Johnny's going to a building and not being feed and y'all are going to stop putting all the blame on a Pastor, Minister, or whoever is preaching, because it's your responsibility to make sure that whereever you are going that you are being fed the word of God and not there to just be there so that people will know you have been to church.

Church services is to teach, uplift, give guidance, improve our spirituality, to live better lives and connect with other Believers, but it's your responsibility to make sure you are in a place being feed.

... work out your salvation ... for it is God who works in you ... Do everything without grumbling or arguing, so that you may become blameless and pure ... Then you will shine... Philippians 2:12-15 NIV

... let your light shine before others, that they may see your good deeds and glorify your Father ... Matthew 5:16 NIV

Do not merely listen to the word, and so deceive yourselves. Do what it says. James 1:22 NIV

... The only thing that counts is faith expressing itself through love. Galatians 5:6 NIV

These passages reveal that a Christian's light is a process of growing in love by faith and cooperation with the Holy Spirit.

Jesus said, "Let your light shine before others" (Matthew 5:16a). He explained that no one lights a lamp just to hide it under a basket. A lamp is meant to be placed on a stand to give light to everything around it. Whether you're timid or outgoing, you're called to be a light to the people around you. So what that means is that if you will allow the spotlight to be on God and not man then your light will shine, but too many of us either want the big light, give it to a man, or woman and give Jesus the little light. Let me ask you Mister and Miss Believer, what have we done to get the big light, I know what Jesus did he died for my sins so I give him the BIG light and I'm completely over-joyed to have that little light and I most certainly don't let anyone else have it

So what does a radiant Christian look like? Is it a person who smiles all the time and never seems to have a bad day? Is it someone who is impressively nice, or the most outwardly generous person you know?

Maybe, or maybe not. Remember day three's soul alignment—our actions and our motives matter.

Take a second to think about this stunningly true quote from the popular book *The Boy, the Mole, the Fox and the Horse*:

"Isn't it odd. We can only see our outsides, but nearly everything happens on the inside."

Radiant love stops looking at the surface. It stops comparing, judging, criticizing, and acting out of prejudice, and instead looks to God.

We shine God's love when we know our battle is against spiritual darkness and we prayerfully fight for unity with other Christ followers. We shine when we speak up and act on behalf of injustices, live generously and gratefully, do all the good we can, and love our enemies.

Secular culture tries to lure us into seeking our own pleasure, philosophy, popularity, and purpose outside of God. Ironically, secularism has created a world of people who are chronically insecure and empty. They have either neglected or rejected exalting and magnifying God.

In contrast, the most God-glorifying people know their identity and significance comes from Him.

Brothers and sisters in Christ, to continually shine Christ's love, we must remember that we are fully secure and infinitely significant through Christ. He is our life, our security, and our significance.

And when we live by His Spirit, secure in who we are in Him, love emanates brilliantly from us, and God receives all the glory.

Scripture Reference

Psalm 34:3
Oh, magnify the LORD with me, and let us exalt his name together!

Blessed are the pure in heart: for they shall see God. Rejoice, and be exceeding glad: for great is your reward in heaven: for so persecuted they the prophets which were before you. Ye are the salt of the earth: but if the salt have lost his savior, wherewith shall it be salted? it is thenceforth good for nothing, but to be cast out, and to be trodden under foot of men. Ye are the light of the world. A city that is set on an hill cannot be hid. Neither do men light a candle, and put it under a bushel, but on a candlestick; and it giveth light unto all that are in the house. Let your light so shine before men, that they may see your good works, and glorify your Father which is in heaven.

Matthew 5:8, 12-16 KJV
But be ye doers of the word, and not hearers only, deceiving your own selves.

Psalm 34:5

O magnify the LORD with me, And let us exalt his name together. I sought the LORD, and he heard me, And delivered me from all my fears. They looked unto him, and were lightened: And their faces were not ashamed."

Loving God Requires Us To Focus On The Things Of God

In the Book of Micah 6:8, listed out the three principles of what God asks of His people: to do justice, to love kindness, and to walk humbly with Him.

Whoever lives in love lives in God, and God in them. This is how love is made complete among us... (1 John 4:10-12,16-17). Receiving the love of God, trusting the love of God, and sharing the love of God is the most important thing for a believer to do

Do nothing out of selfish ambition or vain conceit. Rather, in humility value others above yourselves, not looking to your own interests but each of you to the interests of the others. Philippians 2:3-4.

A growing love is others-oriented. I can't really love you if I'm only focused on me, my approval, my appetite, or my next achievement. So, in order to really love one another, we'll need to truly be concerned about others. Place your focus more on God and his instructions more than what you think you need to do and for God's sake stop letting other people's tell you what they think when God has given you directions!

I believe distraction is a primary weapon of our spiritual enemy. What does our enemy want to distract us from? The answer is anything that matters to God and his direct instructions.

Let's talk about some of the things that cause us to be distracted and lose our focus. For me I have to make sure that no matter how long I have to read in the mornings to do what God's has instructed me to do rather than finishing so that I can go into my weight room to workout. I enjoy the 10-15 minutes after the workout to relax before getting ready for work but sometimes I can't but it's more important to follow God than to chase rest.

Now what are distractions? Anything that draws our attention or mind to something else. Things that takes us away from what we need to be doing rather than what we want to do, and yes sometimes we might think we are doing what's best but make sure that you are doing what God has instructed you to do because I can tell you for sure there have been times I just wanted to do what Vince wanted to do and I landed my butt in so much of a mess that only God could get me out. Let me tell you also why David is probably my favorite person to study, because like David I sometimes think I know what I'm doing but forget to consult God or really listen to the Holy Spirit, but when I realize I'm in a situation I'm willingly admitting it to God and seeking his help, his deliverance, and somewhat accepts his punishment for it but you can bet that I know he still loves me because he ALWAYS SEES ME THROUGH IT!

Scripture Reference

2 Samuel 11:1

In the spring, at the time when kings go off to war, David sent Joab out with the king's men and the whole Israelite army. They destroyed the Ammonites and besieged Rabbah. But David remained in Jerusalem. Now we really don't know why David didn't obey God's instructions, but we do know the outcome was a costly sin that brought great grief into his family.

Numbers 20

Moses turns to God for help and God tells Moses to speak to the rock and water will come out. Instead, Moses hits the rock and as a result he is told he can no longer lead the people into the land of Israel so Moses wasn't allowed to enter into the promised land now I need you to also stop assuming Moses didn't go to heaven I believe that he and David awaits us in heaven just like the rest of the saints but I also believe not following Gods instructions can lead us to some unnecessary hard times.

_____
_____
_____
_____
_____
_____
_____

18

TO GROW IN GOD'S LOVE REQUIRES SOUL ALIGNMENT

To love well we need sincere, pure motivations. Therefore, a growing love needs a healthy self-awareness and soul alignment. Now let's talk about self-awareness for a second what is self-awareness? Knowing and being honest with yourself. Now why is it so important, especially for a Believer?

Self-awareness gives us the potential to become closer to God and become a better versions of ourselves, as God intended.

When we lack self-awareness, we misunderstand ourselves, and that leads to misunderstanding God and others and more importantly it hinders the growth of your relationship with God and others.

Now let's talk a little bit about Soul Alignment:

Soul Alignment is when we align our hearts with God, where our spirits, souls, and bodies work together in peace and harmony.

Soul alignment means finding your place in the world, the source of your power, and becoming more conscious of who you really are and what God requires of you.

I think that was the biggest difference between David as King and Saul as king.

David was able to was able to be honest about his flaws and sin whereas Saul constantly disobeyed God and blamed everyone else. Some of us are living our lives like that today we think we are good people but still justifying all the wrong and sin in our lives rather than being accountable and admitting it's us that need to change. This is something I've learned and share with others God is not going to judge me by how people treat me but he's going to judge me based on how I treat others.

Is your love sincere—meaning without hypocrisy or pretense? How can you know? Take intentional time for soul alignment. Let me explain.

When we can admit and realize that we have absolutely need for God's help when it comes to fully loving Him and others, and being completely honest with ourselves then we can align ourselves up with God's purpose for us and grow in his grace. One of the benefits of daily looking to and relying on God is that He will often reveal something specific that needs correction—or a soul alignment.

Sometimes, God will show me my shortcomings and I will get mad at first and sometimes he has to send someone that's able to talk sense into me and yes that's a difficult job. God really need to pay Sabrina and Val a little extra money but like David I'm quick to repent and ask God to change and strengthen me.

God says we must be aligned with Him before we can be effective anywhere and to anyone else. Our identity is not in our families, our careers, our ministries. God lent us those things, but they are not who we are at our core – God is. If He is not first, He is not on our list

Philippians 4 13?
I can do all things through him who strengthens me.

Colossians 4:12 Prays for Us to Stand Firm

God, I pray that you would help them to stand firm, that you would help them to stand mature and fully assured in your will. Help them to walk in your will. God, as they face temptations today. That you would help them to turn from those temptations. Growing In God's Love requires not knowing everything

Now I've been accused of being a know it all but when it comes to God, I'm humbling confessing that I'm still learning.

With God I'm continuing to grow in knowledge and understanding of God and to understand his purpose for us and to gain with him requires us to be humble without pride and without being a know it all.

Here's the thing: Learning is good. We especially need to grow in our knowledge of God's Word! But there are some problems with knowledge sometimes God gives us a little knowledge to understand certain things then we forget it was God that gave us the ability to have knowledge and understand and we become to prideful and loss ourselves in people praises. Now I'm constantly being told that God is really using me, but I completely understand that I'm only his tool and

I'm constantly checking Pride and the know it all attitude when dealing with God.

I need you to consider the big problems with knowledge:

We can too easily depend on knowledge instead of God and we can become proud and defensive of our knowledge. Pride and love do not coexist.

So to truly love God and have true knowledge we must lose Pride.

Proverbs 11:2 "When pride comes, then comes disgrace, but with humility comes wisdom." Proverbs 16:5 "The LORD detests all the proud of heart. Be sure of this: They will not go unpunished." Proverbs 16:18 "Pride goes before destruction, a haughty spirit before a fall." Growing In God's Love Requires Not Knowing Everything

I've been accused of being a know it all, but when it comes to God, I'm humbling confessing that I'm still learning.

With God I'm continuing to grow in knowledge and understanding of God and to understand his purpose for us and to gain with him requires us to be humble without pride and without being a know it all.

Here's the thing: Learning is good. We especially need to grow in our knowledge of God's Word! But there are some problems with knowledge sometimes God gives us a little knowledge to understand certain things then we forget it was God that gave us the ability to have knowledge and understand and we become to prideful and loss ourselves in people praises. Now I'm constantly being told that God is really using me but I completely understand that I'm only his tool and

I'm constantly checking Pride and the know it all attitude when dealing with God.

Here's the thing that I need you to consider the big problems with knowledge:

We can too easily depend on knowledge instead of God.

We can become proud and defensive of our knowledge and pride and love do not coexist.

So to truly love God and to have true knowledge we must lose Pride.

Scripture Reference

Proverbs 11:2

When pride comes, then comes disgrace, but with humility comes wisdom.

Proverbs 16:5

The LORD detests all the proud of heart. Be sure of this: They will not go unpunished.

Proverbs 16:18 "

Pride goes before destruction, a haughty spirit before a fall.

_____
_____
_____
_____

19

SOMETIMES WE HAVE TO PUSHING OUR WAY PAST OUR PAIN

Now I know that sounds like something I would tell the kids that I train in basketball or weightlifting, but as a Believer in Christ sometimes we have to push ourselves past our pain to get where God wants us to be but don't worry you are not alone.

1 Chronicles 28:20 David also said to Solomon his son, "Be strong and courageous, and do the work. Do not be afraid or discouraged, for the LORD God, my God, is with you. He will not fail you or forsake you until all the work for the service of the temple of the LORD is finished.

Genesis 28:15 I am with you and will watch over you wherever you go, and I will bring you back to this land. I will not leave you until I have done what I have promised you."

Revelation 3:10 Since you have kept my command to endure patiently, I will also keep you from the hour of trial that is going to come on the whole world to test the inhabitants of the earth.

Now a couple of things that I want to hit on this morning: As Believers we need to stop saying that was in the Bible days and stop reading or thinking God's words, God's healing, God's deliverance, God's punishment, God's love, God's forgiveness, God's commandments and God's blessings only applied to the people you read about in the Bible, it's for you, it's your road map, your guide to God so get it off the shelf and read it.

Now let talk about

1 Corinthians 10 vs 13

No temptation has overtaken you except what is common to mankind. And God is faithful; he will not let you be tempted beyond what you can bear. But when you are tempted, he will also provide a way out so that you can endure it.

Too many people take this and run with it and get it completely wrong. The Bible does not teach that "God won't give you more than you can handle." Many believers claim that 1 Corinthians 10:13 teaches "God won't give you more than you can handle." This verse states, "No temptation has overtaken you that is not common to man. Now think about this for a second, if God didn't allow us to go through more than we can bear Jesus would not have died on the Cross for our sins, we would have been able to handle it. If we didn't go through more than we can bear, Jesus would not have left the Holy Spirit here to watch over us and guide us the problem is we don't listen or trust the Holy Spirit enough to follow his instructions and as soon as something goes wrong instead of depending on, following and trusting God, Jesus, and The Holy Spirit. We start looking for ways out of our situations ourselves sometimes you just push yourself past your pain, your hurt, your disappointments, and trust God to deliver you past the things that you cannot bare but you are going to have to keep pushing and believing not complaining and giving up.

I'm not saying it's going to be easy. It's a process, sometimes a long one. As Believers we want a quick fix but with God it's a process. So keep pray and keep believing but here's the thing while you are pushing your way through gain Godly strength and Godly wisdom. You have to learn that your weapons are not physical, but your battle is a Spiritual Battle so we have to use Spiritual Weapons, The Bible, The prayer, The trust, The belief and The endurance to push your way through.

Guys you are not alone and you don't have to bare this by yourself so relax.

Scripture Reference

Psalm 116:7

Return to your rest, O my soul, for the Lord has dealt bountifully with you.

1 Peter 5:6-7

Therefore humble yourselves under the mighty hand of God, that He may exalt you in due time, casting all your care upon Him, for He cares for you.

Psalm 62:5

My soul, wait silently for God alone, for my expectation is from Him.

Provers 19:23

The fear of the Lord leads to life; then one rests content, untouched by trouble.

20

Your Focus Is Required to Love

What is love? Love is an emotion that keeps people bonded and committed to one another.

Now what is Godly love? To understand the attitudes and actions of godly love requires far, far more revelation than knowing the definitions of a couple of Greek words and a couple of Hebrew words. Godly love is a spiritual love that God through His Holy Spirit enables us to have (Romans 5:5; Galatians 5:22; 1 John 4:7-13)

Everything we become or have experienced comes from love or lack of love and either way you will be hurt, confused, overwhelmed, happy, find joy and laughter sometimes with the same people.

Now I can tell you with certainty that when you love and you are hurt, offended and mistreated when loving that God will always be in a place to heal your heart and bring good out of the situation.

Now if you are anything like me you have loved someone that has taken that love for granted and made it difficult to love again so the question

I will ask you is the same question I've asked myself several times, why do we still look for love?

I think it's because we know that love teaches us so many of life lessons and our love for God teaches us to continue to even love the people that misuse and mistreat us. Now I know this sounds like a old cliché, but I believe we learn more of how to love from people that mistreated us than the ones that love us, we actually learn what love ain't in order to learn what love is and more importantly than our love with people it teaches us how to love God more but the more important thing that I've learned is that it teaches me why God loves me so much even though I've taken his love for granted, misused and mistreated him. He still waits in a place to lift me up from the situations, the circumstances that I sometimes put myself in.

Have you ever just wondered why God continues to protect, provide and deliver you even from the mess you make of your own lives sometimes? It's called LOVE.

Love is a weapon that can shatter, divide and tear down especially our hearts but when we have God's love it's a weapon that builds, brings unity, mends and brings joy.

Our ability to love God with all our heart, soul, mind, and strength is not only a commandment but also a gateway to a life filled with blessings, guidance, peace, purpose, and eternal hope. It teaches us how to love and accept love from others.

Scripture Reference

1 John 4:7-8.

Dear friends, let us love one another, for love comes from God. Everyone who loves has been born of God and knows God.

What Season Are You In?

All seasons of life until eternal life are part of living out God's plan for our lives. Ecclesiastes 3:1 reads, To everything there is a season, and a time to every purpose under the heaven. Notice the repetition of "every" as well as "time": "season" is a Hebrew word that is literally "appointed time".

What I'm learning is our attitude, beliefs, trust, and determination determines our seasons. Let me see if I can explain: I don't care who you are, you will find yourself in some kind of situation that's difficult and it's usually a situation that you don't feel like you deserve to be going through. You have to understand this the Devil ain't looking for the ones that he already got, he's looking to destroy the ones that belong to God but the good news is he can't have you.

If you are anything like me you have asked God why does he even allow Satan to bring conflict in our lives especially with our families?

Let's talk about 5 encouraging lessons during the seasons of conflict.

First, I have discovered an astonishing truth: God is attracted to our weakness. When we are empty vessels, He longs to fill us with His grace, love and goodness. An empty vessel is what God desires so He can fill you with what you will need for the season you are in. In times when there is great stress or conflict you need extra doses of grace, love and goodness. You will also need more faith.

Secondly It's a season . . . not a sentence. This too shall pass, and when the storm has passed, only the harshest of words spoken will be remembered. So when you are in the heat of the moment, it is critical that you guard your tongue: "Death and life are in the power of the tongue" (Proverbs 18:21). I'm still learning because I will be honest with you sometimes I want to do the Angie with people, that's my sister the one that if you bother me, you are going to get a lot of cuss words thrown at you, words that you almost have to fight after hearing!

Third, the pain that you feel is pain that you will heal from when you give it over to God. I know sometimes when people bring me the things that they are going through they feel like I'm not concerned enough I didn't pray enough with them but as your brother in Christ, as someone that God chose sometimes I have to wait on a word from God but I pray for each of you guys often. Sometimes it's even difficult for me to watch you go through what you are going through even when God tells me he got this.

Fourth, never underestimate the power of being in God's presence and I believe when we go to the house of God things change now when I say the house of God. I need you to understand there's a difference between the house of God and a building, the house of Gods is the man or woman of God that God chose to deliver his message the building is just where they are in. house.

Besides the Word of God, there are also the people of God—relationships that develop when people are together week after week over an extended period of time. And you never know when there will be that breakthrough moment. There are some amazing things that happens when God children are gathered together especially when one of them has the gift to preach his word, a couple of weeks ago I had breakfast with my anointed brothers and sister and I could feel God's presence in the place.

Lastly, and most important of all, never forget, love matters. It really does.

A New Language

Love does cover a multitude of sins and speaks a language all its own. In everything that you go through stress, conflict, depression, disappointments, betrayal. None of these things will outweigh the fact that God loves you and has every intention of protecting, delivering and blessing you but we must continue on our journey with him doing what he has called us to do and be where he has assigned us to be and listening to his words from the people that he has chosen to share his words, to pray over you and to pray for you.

Life is an adventure in forgiveness. It's all about releasing the past and reaching for the future. And I know of only one way to do this: Love like you have never been hurt and trust God with all.

Scripture Reference

"And above all things have fervent love for one another, for 'love will cover a multitude of sins'" (1 Peter 4:8)

LEARN TO FORGIVE AND LET GO TO HEAL

Have You ever wondered why Jesus was able to forgive even when he was on the cross and he said

I have often wondered how Jesus was able to remain forgiving and compassionate to the very end, especially when you consider the lies, betrayal, injustice, false accusation and sheer hatred directed toward Him.

Now I have often told people that there's no way I could have be Jesus up on that cross and stayed there forgiving then it was presented to me like this, what if it was your children, someone that you wanted to be saved would you not only be willing to forgive but also die for them?

There's so much to learn about God and his complete plan for your life, one of the things that I'm learning is as we wait on him we have to wait in expectation believe he's going to do exactly what he said he would do. Jesus was able to do what was necessary even through all that pain because he was waiting expectingly on God to do what he said he would do.

I also think that sometimes we go through unnecessary things because not only because of our sins of omission rather than our sins of commission.

A sin of commission involves the willful act of doing something that violates God's commands in Scripture, such as lying or stealing. A sin of omission involves not doing what is right or failing to do as instructed. As I study God's word, I realize so many of us failed and are still failing God more for our sins of omission. What would have happened if Jesus had to decided nope I ain't doing this? What would have happened to Joseph's family if he had decided I don't care what the king dreamed and who can't interpret it I've been stuck here in prison, and no one helped me so I ain't doing nothing? Moses didn't make it to the promise land because of sin of omission, while Although David did catch hell, but he remained King. Now understand I'm not telling one sin is worse than another, but I just believe even at our worst when we continue to wait expectingly on God, he changes your situation. As long as Job was complaining his situation didn't change, has God ever had to remind you of who he is and it's his plan, his purpose like he did Job, he's had to so many times with me, I really can't count them, I remember how I was complaining and not praying about a situation to God and he stopped me right in the middle of my whining and said Vince, so when he says Vince that means he's not that mad at me but now when he calls me hey you then I'm in trouble but he said Vince have you talked to me about it or do you think the whining is going to fix it? So I shut up and started praying and so here's the thing I prayed waiting and expecting God to move and he did. It wasn't until Job stop feeling sorry for himself and stopped whining about his situation and then God told him to pray for the ones that were constantly accusing him, God even convicted them by letting them know that you been judging Job when there are things that you need to be delivered from so I need you to get Job to pray for you. We will deal with adversity, hurts, mistreatment and unhappiness as Believers but I just believe our seasons of blessings, deliverance and happiness is controlled by our attitudes and our ability to wait expectingly on God.

What does it really mean to wait expectingly on God?

That means we don't fret or wait fearfully. We wait, expecting God to engage in our world while faith fills our soul with expectation and we must listen to and obey what the Holy Spirit tells you about a situation because when Jesus ascended into heaven, he didn't leave us here alone, we have the Holy Spirit with us the problems are we sometimes get to caught up in our whining our woe is me attitude rather than listening to what the Holy Spirit is telling us, don't you hate to tell someone something that you know will help them but they keep doing something else, I'm just glad that the Holy Spirit has more patience with me than I have with people.

Scripture Reference

Luke 23:34
Then said Jesus, Father, forgive them; for they know not what they do. And they parted his raiment, and cast lots.

_____

_____

23

LETTING GO TO GAIN

Too many times we can't hold the things that God wants to bless our lives with because we are still holding on to the things that hurt us. Unforgiveness, bitterness, anger, offense, hurt and injustice can and will have a damaging effect on our spirits. These effects disrupt our spiritual health and can harm our physical health as well. Many times I know that when we have placed our trust in someone and they hurt, destroy and play with your feelings it makes you not only not trust people but you want to close up your heart to love.

Now I don't recommend or desire for anyone to go through the pain of finding out that someone you placed your trust in or someone that you loved and you heart was destroyed in the process but there's a lesson even in those unfortunate times.

The Bible tells us that God is asking all of His people to live on a higher level than the nonbeliever. The Bible tells us to forgive those who will trespass against us, to turn the other cheek if warranted, to love our enemies, and to do good to those who will deliberately hurt us. Now if you are like me then my question to God is why?

Because while pain and suffering are never enjoyable, God often allows them in our lives because he loves us so much, he is willing to allow us to experience short term problems so we will reap long-term pleasures in him. Oftentimes nothing awakens us and causes us to seek God's presence more than pain and to be honest I've learned more about God through my pain and when the blessing comes I'm better at using them for us glory.

Guys I didn't really want to go back to Joseph this soon but do you really think he would have been prepared for his calling from God had he not gone through the things that he went through?

Let me tell you about me I knew that God had a calling on my life so I ran because I knew there were things that I was going to need to give up no not those things, I knew that I would have to learn to live through some suffering and still love, so mistreatment and still love, some broken trust issues and still love. Because there's no way around it for a Believer.

Suffering causes our focus to turn inward, to face those parts of ourselves we might otherwise ignore. Now the Devil means it to separate us and to destroy our love for God and other but God uses our suffering to develop a better you to teach us how to use what he's blessed us with to also help others.

God allowed me to be the vessel in a sermon that he did about Ruth.

How she followed her mother in-law back to her people even though her husband had died. So when Ruth got there she went to work in Boaz field with his servant and he told them to leave things behind so that she would have enough when you have God's anointing and favor He will put the RIGHT people in your path. Now God gave me this vision of the night before Ruth was to go and work in the field of what was her blessing Ruth knew she was going to need something to gather up her blessings I can just see Ruth looking in her basket now it was full of things from her past that she knew she didn't need like hurt, mistreatment, suffering, loneliness, struggles, stress, sin, pain and loss and lack of love. See Ruth understood she needed to get rid of those things to make room for all the blessings that God had for her, some of us can't move forward to our blessings because we got our basket full of things carrying them around things that we not only don't need but also things that God has delivered us from but we won't move forward to our blessings we keep looking backwards running into problems. Now I can just see Ruth now as she's working now I believe in the beginning she was worried about all the things she left behind but I just believe as she continued to do what God had told her to do she picked up happiness on the trail, she picked up Joy on the trail, she picked him deliverance on the trail, she picked up trust on the trail. I see her now with tears in our eyes as she thought about all that God had kept her through all the hurt, all the disappointments and the suffering but when she learned to leave all that behind see apparently Boaz was watching her now I'm better sure he was like most of us men, he saw something he liked in the physical because men don't lie, when we first saw our wives it was something about how they looked that got our attention but what kept us is something deeper, Boaz saw what God was blessing him with a strong fighter someone that not only loved God but was willing to do whatever she needed to do to please God not with words but with her life and he wanted that blessing in his life.

And Ruth never lower her standards to find love or happiness we know that Boaz married and Ruth bore him a son, Obed, who became the father of Jesse, the father of King David.

SCRIPTURE REFERENCE

Romans 5:1-3

1 Therefore being justified by faith, we have peace with God through our Lord Jesus Christ:

2 By whom also we have access by faith into this grace wherein we stand, and rejoice in hope of the glory of God.

3 And not only so, but we glory in tribulations also: knowing that tribulation worketh patience;

James 1:2-8

2 My brethren, count it all joy when ye fall into divers temptations;

3 Knowing this, that the trying of your faith worketh patience.

4 But let patience have her perfect work, that ye may be perfect and entire, wanting nothing.

5 If any of you lack wisdom, let him ask of God, that giveth to all men liberally, and upbraideth not; and it shall be given him.

6 But let him ask in faith, nothing wavering. For he that wavereth is like a wave of the sea driven with the wind and tossed.

7 For let not that man think that he shall receive any thing of the Lord.

8 A double minded man is unstable in all his ways.

24

EVERYTHING HAS A SEASON

In Genesis chapter 50, Jacob has died and the scripture begins with his embalming and seventy day period or mourning (as was the custom of the day). In the very first verse we see Joseph throwing himself over his Father, weeping and kissing him. In verse 10 we see the entire extended group lamenting, loudly and bitterly, followed by another week-long period of mourning. It seems that Joseph's family understood a fundamental lesson of life so much better than we do in our world today: life has seasons.

The Word of God, teach us that life has its seasons. We see it in everything around us from the flowers, the weather, our music, our clothes, and we see it in the world and our lives. In this Chapter, Joseph and his extended family take their season to mourn. They understand that it won't be forever, but it's what they need to do right now. They understand and embrace its importance. One of the things that I've noticed about families we all mourn differently some of weep with people, some weep in private and sometimes we just need time and space to be able to mourn until we are good.

The perspective of being able to grasp the fact that we have seasons in our lives as Believers is very important to our growth and our faith. I would only hope to be as resilience in my faith, patience and trust as Joseph was with God and people, he was able to see the big picture, he didn't focus on where he was, he focused on where he is going. I believe the reason some of us haven't grown into what God wants us to be is because we are holding on to a season that's over. God has opened the door to your blessings, but we haven't changed in understanding our seasons of struggle is over that if we will only walk just a little further with him, we will find our seasons of blessings, what I've found out in this life and studying God's word our seasons of blessings never leaves, it our outlook that determines our outcome. Let me ask this question: who was more in bondage by what Joseph's brothers did to him, Joseph or them? Yes Joseph was surrounded by walls at times and left in a unknown land but was he ever really in bondage see everything and everywhere he went God blessed it but his brother were constantly going through things now the walls that surrounded them was sin and I can tell you for certain there's no greater bondage than living away from God because when we live in sin we live a hopeless life but when we live for God, we understand that no weapon formed against you shall prosper and no matter what people try and do to you, you are living in your season of blessings. Your attitude, your trust and your belief determine your season. I choose God and my season to be blessed even in the midst of storms.

When we flee from temptation, practice patience, walk in humility, express emotional maturity, forgive those who hurt us, trust God and see life as a blessing our seasons of blessings, our resilience will grow as will our godliness grows.

Scripture Reference

Ecclesiastes 3:1-8

a time to be born, and a time to die;

a time to plant, and a time to pluck up what is planted;

a time to kill, and a time to heal;

a time to break down, and a time to build up;

a time to weep, and a time to laugh;

a time to mourn, and a time to dance;

a time to cast away stones, and a time to gather stones together;

a time to embrace, and a time to refrain from embracing;

a time to seek, and a time to lose;

a time to keep, and a time to cast away;

a time to tear, and a time to sew;

a time to keep silence, and a time to speak;

a time to love, and a time to hate;

a time for war, and a time for peace."

_____

_____

Our Forgiveness Allows Us to Find God

What is Forgiveness? Jesus says forgiveness is an action that is intentionally taken (Luke 17:3); the sinned-against person hears/sees the action of repentance and responds.

To not forgive is transgression against God when we refuse to forgive those who have repented for their offenses to us. This is the teaching of Jesus. It is the mandate of Jesus. As we are united in Christ, we are to show that union by extending the same grace to others that He extends to us.

When Joseph sees his brothers he's overcome with emotion. So much so that his loud weeping becomes a point of gossip and conversation, we see that In Genesis 45:2.

Now understand this Joseph was sold into slavery by his own family (but to be fair, they were going to kill him, and so I guess that's a better alternative??). He was falsely accused, and then imprisoned for several years. And yet the LORD had used him in mighty ways! The LORD had given Joseph gifts to use to save a lot of people and mind you the very ones that mistreated him but instead of holding a grudge or seeking revenge he used his gift and position for good too many times we think now that we are in charge or have the upper hand, we are going to let everybody know this world is mine! But instead, time and time again we see that because the LORD was with him, he had the ability to overcome some truly terrible circumstances, displaying great resilience through his fleeing of temptation, his practice of patience, his humility, and his emotionally mature response to incredibly charged and difficult circumstances, and because of that God not only blessed him but his entire family was saved and blessed so you can imagine how much love and respect he had from his two sons because of his ability to trust God through everything.

Everything thus far has led up to today's chapter, where Joseph reveals his identity to his brothers.

We can learn a lot from Joseph here: having a God perspective of our lives changes everything, and leading with forgiveness opens us up not only to become truly resilient people, but those who are in tune with the very heart of God.

I'm learning in this stage of my life that being blessed isn't the absence of problems but it's the presence of God and knowing that no weapon formed against us shall prosper that God has a way of taking the things that people try to do to us and turn them around what they meant for our bad God brings the good out of our situations. Forgive often and Love always.

Scripture Reference

Luke 6:37-38

Judge not, and ye shall not be judged: condemn not, and ye shall not be condemned: forgive, and ye shall be forgiven: give, and it shall be given unto you; good measure, pressed down, and shaken together, and running over, shall men give into your bosom. For with the same measure that ye mete withal it shall be measured to you again.

26

EMOTIONS ARE NOT YOUR ENEMY BUT NEITHER SHOULD THEY BE YOUR GUIDE

Just as the LORD had shown Joseph in his dream there was a great famine in the land. There was not enough food and people were starving. Many people traveled great distances to find anything to eat and feed their families.

In chapters 42-45, we read that this was also the case for Joseph's family. Now let's think about this for a second these same brothers that sold him, parted him from his father and youngster brother were their asking for food.

God has a way of bringing those very people that mistreated you back to needing you.

Acts 2:35 Until I make thy foes thy footstool. Now that doesn't mean that you are supposed to mistreat them or how grudge's God don't need your help in judging or punishing someone you do what God has requirements of you to do.

A lot happens within these passages, and Joseph sees his brothers several times. He learns that he is father and youngest brother Benjamin is alive and well but Joseph had a opportunity to learn something that a lot of us as Believers need to learn that what God has for you is for you that no one can stop what God has ordained or blessed you with and when they throw obstacles in your path I just believe two things happens you learn to appreciate God more on your journey and he also strengthens you on your journey.

There were a series of emotions involved in the reuniting of Joseph with his family, Regret (42:22), Weeping (42:24, 43:30), Sinking hearts (42:28), Fright (42:35, 43:18), Bereavement (43:14), Being deeply moved (43:30), among others! And Romans 12:19

Do not take revenge, my dear friends, but leave room for God's wrath, for it is written: "It is mine to avenge; I will repay," says the Lord.

The key to resilience is emotional maturity. We must learn to simultaneously embrace (and not stuff) our emotions, at the same time as not being ruled by them.

Now for some of us this does not come naturally we have to work hard at it. I can't tell you how many times after getting into a fight, my mom would get onto me and I would always say they started it. I just finished it. She would tell me to let God handle it but I thought that I was helping God but what I was really doing is putting myself in a position to miss my blessings, Joseph could have easily taken revenge on everyone that mistreated him but we need to understand what we went through as a lesson but also appreciate God for keeping us and use it as a stepping stone to get where God wants us to be, if we hold on to the emotion of anger and revenge then our hands are too full to hold our blessings, our deliverance and our relationship with God.

This something you are naturally good at, or is it an area in which you need to grow? How is emotional maturity modelled in your family, in a healthy way, or in an unhealthy way?

Let's ask the Lord for wisdom in how to add emotional maturity to our list of resilience keys. We must become people who flee from temptation, practice patience, walk in humility, and grow in emotional maturity.

Scripture Reference

Philippians 4:6

Do not be anxious about anything, but in everything by prayer and supplication with t

thanksgiving let your requests be made known to God."

Ephesians 4:26-27

"Be angry and do not sin; do not let the sun go down on your anger, and give no opportunity to the devil."

Proverbs 29:11

"A fool gives full vent to his spirit, but a wise man quietly holds it back."

Proverbs 16:32

"Whoever is slow to anger is better than the mighty, and he who rules his spirit than he who takes a city."

27

It Belongs To God

One of the things that I truly love about Joseph is that I know he's a better man than me, I'm still growing in some of the areas that he mastered.

I mean think, being sold into slavery, falsely imprisoned, forgotten about with no end in sight (for two years!), and then Pharaoh (the Pharaoh) has a dream.

In Genesis 41, we read the details of Pharaoh's two dreams. Nobody in all the land could interpret them. This mystery jogs the memory of the cupbearer (about time!) and all of a sudden Joseph is freed from his cell and finds himself in front of Egypt's King.

Too many times we want the credit or be put up on a pedestal for a Spiritual Gift that God gave us rather than give him the credit, when in John 12:32 he tells us And I, if I be lifted up from the earth, will draw all men unto me. So when God is lifted up for the Spiritual Gifts that you have received instead of that stuff we like to do stick out your chest and take all the credit then he continues to bless you with more if you use those correctly.

Now I've been told that sometimes my messages are too long and sometimes they are too short but the messages goes out to a lot of people and also I have to start back doing sermons as well now I want everybody to know I hear you and because God said to I will but I always want you to credit God not Vince because I can tell you for sure these Spiritual Gifts belong to God and not me.

Now let's go back to Joseph gives God the credit He is due, and stands firm within today's key to building a life of resilience: humility.

Humility is the absence of pride or arrogance. It's having a modest view of your own self-importance. It is, as C.S. Lewis so eloquently put it:

"Humility is not thinking less of yourself, it's thinking of yourself less."

Because of his humble response, and in an incredible twist of circumstances, Joseph goes from being in prison to being second-in-command over the entire land of Egypt. In one swift move he traded his chains for chariots and went from rags to robes. He victoriously walked the fine line between being confident in the power of God, but humble in his own self.

Joseph teaches us so many valuable lessons here: give God the glory, for it is His. Stand in humility, as well as in His power and later on he shows humility and forgiveness towards his brothers even before they ask for his forgiveness, he tells them they meant it for bad but God meant it for their good.

Once again, we often do not choose our circumstances, but we always have the choice of our response and we become resilient people when we flee from temptation, practice patience, and walk in humility with God.

In all that we do glorify God not man and most certainly not ourselves.

We become meek and teachable like a child. In Matthew 18:4; We overcome pride and "recognize gratefully our dependence on the Lord." 1 We repent when we need to repent. We understand that we need Heavenly Father's support and that our talents and our gifts come from Him.

Scripture Reference

Genesis 41:15

Pharaoh said to Joseph, "I have had a dream, and there is no one who can interpret it. I have heard it said of you that when you hear a dream you can interpret it" and in response, now in verse 16, Joseph says "I cannot do it... but God will give Pharaoh the answer he desires."

_____
_____
_____
_____
_____
_____
_____
_____

28

FLEEING FROM TEMPTATION

Now I think most of you know the story about Joseph's brother being so jealous of his relationship with his father, but I also want you to know this they also knew what the father knew and what Joseph knew that God was with Joseph. Now let me see if I can help you to understand what that really means when God is with you.

It means that there's nothing that happens that's not a apart of God's ultimate purpose and purpose for your life, that God is with you and has something special in plans for your future when we surrendered to the lordship of Jesus. God, in the person of the Holy Spirit, is with us in a very personal and intimate way. The God of all creation lives within me.

He WILL do what He chooses through you. But when we refuse to obey him that's when we miss his reward of His grace and glory. If you continue to refuse to acknowledge Him and seek Him. When God is with us, He leads us to an ultimate place of blessing that makes the trials fade away.

Here's the thing that I also need you to understand, just as sure as God is getting ready to use you to be a blessing you had better know that Satan is going to put all kinds of temptations in your path, and he's very crafty, it's usually something that you think that you can control but let me tell you this there's absolutely no SIN that we have control over. Do you think a drug addict wanted to be out there in the streets spending all their money and their families money on drugs, do you think that person that's an alcoholic was intend to be out there drunk out of their minds, do you think that compulsive liar intended to continue to lie or that person that has a sex addiction really happy giving up their bodies to someone that they know cares not for them and they don't have feelings for that person?

It all starts with the Power of Fleeing which doesn't happen by accident you have to purposely remove yourself from that situation now here's the thing you have to willingly remove yourself because I don't care how many times you tell yourself I couldn't help myself you are only lying to you because I can tell you for certain each time you find yourself in a situation the Holy Spirit will warn us but here the problem when you don't remove yourself from the situation you will get caught up in the situation.

Now let me tell you the difference between what Joseph did and what David did stay with me through this

Joseph master's wife (how's that for a mouthful) persistently tempts and urges Joseph to sin. But he refuses, holding firmly to his beliefs even when she ripped his clothes off he FLEED, he didn't stay there to see what she was working with, see sometimes we have to leave a situation before the situation convinces us that NOBODY WILL KNOW!

Now let's talk about David, first of all when God has given you your instructions under no circumstances do you let anybody tell you something different see we have those so called friends that want to keep you out there in misery because misery loves company and sometimes to keep you out there benefits them.

If David had gone to war with his men like he was told to he wouldn't have been on the roof, now let me say this because I know some of you ask why was he on the roof in the first place, if you will go to the New Testament he will see where Peter was also on the roof, apparently that was the place where they went to think, now Kelvin thought it was strange that his secret place was in the bathroom but guys that's one of the places I go and if Cali is here she will ask Papa why you be in there so long not because she needs to get in there because we are blessed with other bathrooms but that's my buddy and we will sit next to one another doing nothing but we enjoy it but I know that I have to give God his time first. Now the difference between Joseph and David was Joseph fled and David stayed up on that roof with Satan watching Bathsheba take a bath and guys if you don't flee from sin you will flee to sin because David didn't stop there he had someone to bring her to the palace and slept with her but that wasn't enough he had her husband to go into battle so he would get killed so he got Uriah's wife but let me also tell you how much hell David caught after that his children starting fighting and killing one another, one son raped his stepsister and one of them tried to kill David now all of this first because he didn't do what God told him to do and fled to temptation instead of doing like Joseph now I know we see Joseph situation for doing right as a punishment because he went to jail for doing right but let me ask you this who had a rougher time David running for his life with those dysfunctional children or Joseph in the prison running things, see even in prison Joseph was still being blessed and because he was obedient God blessed him with so much more. Guys it one thing to be a man after God's own heart but we must also flee from temptation.

Lead us not into temptation! Pray this over yourself today (and everyday!). A tremendous part of becoming a resilient person is to flee from temptation, just as we see Joseph doing. This is something we can do because the Lord is with us. It's also important to note that fleeing is an active verb. You don't flee accidentally, or subtly. It takes intention, it takes a decision, and it takes action. We must intentionally decide to flee from the temptation(s) that surround us. Like

Joseph we have no control over our circumstances, but we have every control over how we response to them.

Scripture Reference

Luke 11:2-8

Father,

Hallowed be Your name,

Your kingdom come.

Give us each day our daily bread.

Forgive us our sins,

For we also forgive everyone who sins against us.

And lead us not into temptation.

29

THE HARDSHIPS OF BEING FAVORED

In our lifetimes we will face pain and challenges that are inevitable, but there is nothing like the pain or challenges we face as one of God's favorites. Let me try and elaborate on that when God has a calling on your life, when God has picked you out to bless you with a certain gift or anointing then you can rest assure someone will envy that relationship that you have with God and will do everything they can to destroy you and your relationship with God. When I was a fool out there in the world just doing anything. I thought that I was grown enough to do people loved me or feared me but when God convinced and delivered me from all of that foolishness the very people that I thought were my friends started talking about me talking about what I used to do.

The longer I live the more I realize that jealousness has got to be the worst hate there is and most times it comes from the very people that should love you and be in your corner. Let me say this before I go farther into this lesson: People we have got to stop being mad when God bless our sisters and brothers and learn to rejoice and celebrate with them.

You would think after seeing the world in wars, pandemics and disasters in our state and country, within our families, and within our own hearts and lives. We also see it scattered over and over again throughout history, as the story of humanity too often tells the tale of pain and devastation that we would come together and pray but instead looks like we are farther apart.

Now I understand that all these things are a part of life but as a Believer that shouldn't apply to you but unfortunately we sometimes can be the worst ones but it's also funny we a person gives me the excuse that they don't go to church because there's already enough devil's in the church so you be the exception.

The truth is, pain is part of being human. It's part of the common ground that we all share. Therefore, what sets us apart from one another is not the presence of challenges within our lives, but how we respond to them. It is our response that determines not only the kind of life that we lead, but also in turn the kind of people we are and are becoming.

Please read this part very carefully: positive qualities and good character produces positive outcomes. When we continue to serve God with a humble and positive spirit, we can rest assured that the end results will be positive see to many of us, yes I'm guilty we come unglued ready for war as soon as someone test us. When sometimes we need to have the patience of Joseph not Job, see Job got so mad he wanted God to come talk to him so he could tell God about himself how God knew he didn't deserve to be going through what he was going through but when God did have that conversation with Job, it was Job that got straightened out, now God and I have had that very conversation and yep same thing, I had to shut up and listen, but guys instead of Joseph walking around bad at the world he continued with a positive attitude serving God and all of his enemies were placed under his footstool but the most amazing thing he didn't tell them. Look at me now, he even cared for the very ones that mistreated him.

God has a way of turning things around for you but we can't see which way to go because we keep walking with our heads down defeated. There's something that God is getting ready to do in someone life but you have to approach your situation with a positive attitude.

Scripture Reference

Philippians 4:8
Finally, brothers and sisters, whatever is true, whatever is noble, whatever is right, whatever is pure, whatever is lovely, whatever is admirable—if anything is excellent or praiseworthy—think about such things.

Isaiah 41:10-11
10 Fear thou not; for I am with thee: be not dismayed; for I am thy God: I will strengthen thee; yea, I will help thee; yea, I will uphold thee with the right hand of my righteousness.

11 Behold, all they that were incensed against thee shall be ashamed and confounded: they shall be as nothing; and they that strive with thee shall perish.

_____

_____

Learning How To Let It Go

Some many of us can't enjoy life because we are either holding on to past hurts, or feeling guilty or ashamed because of how we used to live but I'm telling you in order to become who God has called you to be we have to learn to let some things GO, that means completely let them GO!

In 2 Corinthians 5:17

Therefore if any man be in Christ, he is a new creature: old things are passed away; behold, all things are become new. That means we will no longer be held accountable for our past sins. It means our old lives are dead and gone. It means the Holy Spirit dwells within us. And I'm telling you it's impossible to hold your blessings, your happiness, your joy and your deliverance when you are trying to also hold on to things that God has already delivered you from.

In Philippians 2:15 says, "Live clean, innocent lives as children of God, shining like bright lights in a world full of crooked and perverse people".

Now I know some of us have a lot that we need God to forgive us for and a lot that he still has to teach us to let go of but I want you to know that the good news is he's just waiting on you.

In Psalm 32:1-2 says: "What happiness for those whose guilt has been forgiven! What joys when sins are covered over! What relief for those who have confessed their sins and God has cleared their record"

Happiness, joy, and relief are three things everybody is looking for. We all want to be happy. We all want to enjoy life. We all want relief from our pain. The Bible says it all comes from purity, and purity comes from forgiveness through God's grace. Not from living a perfect life because I have news for you there's only one that's perfect and that's the Father, so I'm telling you to stop worrying, start praying, stop holding on to what somebody did to you all they really did was helped you to Christ and stop holding onto your past mistakes, if you have wronged someone apologize and LET IT Go

So how do you keep a clear conscience?

At the beginning and end of each day, do a spiritual inventory. Talk to God about anything standing between you and him, and then release the frustrations from your day.

Scripture Reference

1 John 1:9

He is faithful and just and will forgive us our sins and purify us from all unrighteousness.

Psalm 32:1-2

Blessed is he whose transgression is forgiven, Whose sin is covered. Blessed is the man unto whom the LORD imputeth not iniquity, And in whose spirit there is no guile.

Attitude Of Gratefulness

Believers we have to start living a life of gratitude, too many of us are walking around bad with the world, mad at what God is doing in someone else's life instead of being grateful for what he's doing in your life. Your outcome is determined by first your relationship with God and your attitude while living for him, too many of us can't appreciate what he's doing in our lives because we are more concerned with what we think someone else has. Think about this Cain killed his brother not because of what he had but because his relationship wasn't the same as the relationship that Abel had with God. Your blessings are determined by your attitude, gratitude, and your obedience to God, so it's time to stop blaming the world when things are not going the way you wanted them to it's time to look at you. Yes I would be the first person to tell you that sometimes good people go through some bad situations I can witness to that but let me ask you this question are you truly trusting God with a attitude of gratefulness or are you walking around being defeated or in Cain case bad at someone else because of their relationship and obedience to God's word?

The More You look for reasons to be grateful the happier your life becomes and we you learn to focus on the positive rather than the negative so many amazing things happens in your life.

It took me a long time to truly understand why Job, why I dealt with so much adversity in life, as long as we focused on what was wrong with our lives the more we couldn't appreciate what God was doing in our lives, let's go back to the beginning of the book of Job. He often prayed to God about worrying about protecting his children and all of his stuff now understand this we all have concerns and some worry, but it wasn't until Job learned to stop focusing on what he didn't have but when he realized that he had the one thing that Satan couldn't touch was his ability to depend on God not to blame God, he started praying for those so called judge mental friends of his, God not only blessed him but he restored and multiplied to his life.

Gratitude refers to the ability to show thanks for the things you have and the things you're grateful for. It helps you get closer to God by recognizing all the blessings in your life and it makes it easier to focus on the positive. Sometimes we just have to be thankful for what we have because when you focus on the who (God) and the what (life) it truly gets better.

SCRIPTURE REFERENCE

Philippians 4:6-7 - 6
Do not be anxious about anything, but in every situation, by prayer and petition, with thanksgiving, present your requests to God.

Hebrews 12:28

Therefore, since we receive a kingdom which cannot be shaken, let us show gratitude, by which we may offer to God an acceptable service with.

32

LEARNING TO FORGIVE

Guys I still think one of the hardest things for us to do is to forgive people that have mistreated, misused, and took advantage of us especially the ones that have not even parted their lips to apologize or seems like they could care less about your feelings!

Now the human side of me really wants to get them back, let them know how I feel about it with a few choice of cussing words like my late Uncle Fate. He could cuss a person out so bad it was worse than slapping you but here are the things that I've learned all that does is effects my relationship with God and guys the relationship that I have with God is the most important relationship that I have.

Let me also say this and I not saying because she's my daughter but I think that Val is the most forgiving person that I've ever met. Sometimes I get mad that she doesn't get more upset with people, but I also get a chance to see how through a lot of foolishness she maintains her peace and relationship with God.

Why do you think God doesn't only want you to show mercy to the people you like, or only to people who make showing mercy to them easy? Because it's not really mercy, mercy is fueled by compassion, providing promising glints of light in a darkened world. It's kindness, forward forgiveness, and empathy. Mercy chooses not to be offended, and compassionately sees a hurting heart behind hurtful words. God's mercy is reflected in the cross of Christ, a direct reflection of His love for us. So when we can only give it to the ones we like or make it easy is it really mercy?

So let me see if I can bring clarity, on our journey to Heaven we cannot care hate, resentment or anger with us and to be honest carrying it around is extremely heavy.

Jesus died for our sins, so I think we should be able to forgive those that sinned against us but here's the thing too many of us Believers think that if I forgive them they will do it again, if I forgive them then I'm showing weakness, if I forgive them they have gotten away with mistreating me but let me assure we all will reap what we sow. It took a long time for me to understand that I didn't have to bring pain to the ones that mistreated me, that it's God and only Gods job to judge and deliver punishment and yes when one of God's children is mistreated I can assure you that he's involved in making sure things are taken care of.

But now let's talk about why it's important for you to forgive for yourself, how many times have you had a bad day because of what someone else did something to you or you just can't sleep now because someone said something that hurt your feelings, so now let me also ask this question why?

If we say that we truly trust God, then also trust him enough to forgive we cannot afford to burn the bridge you need to walk across in order to get into heaven. And one way you can show God just how thankful you are for his forgiveness is by extending forgiveness to other people even the ones that haven't asked for forgiveness.

Guys we also have to stop saying that I forgive you but because I'm so glad there wasn't a but with God and sometimes we make it hard for a person to apologize because we want to tell them how much they hurt us, has God told you just how much your sin hurt him or did he just accept our apology of forgiveness?

Scripture Reference

Matthew 6:15

If you refuse to forgive others, your Father will not forgive your sins.

33

WANTING TO BE BETTER

I got excited as soon as I started reading this lesson it's about our blind spots.

Now what are our blind spots those are the areas in our lives where we either don't Recognize there's a need to be a better Believer or the areas that we have lied to ourselves thinking I'm good and it's the rest of the world that needs to be better. See sometimes we want to move according to how we feel and not how God has told us to move. Sometimes we think that we are being punished when God is really trying to move us out of our own selfish ways and thoughts.

This is because we all have blind spots, which are attitudes or weaknesses we cannot see or refuse to see even though they cause conflict with others.

So how can you see beyond your self-deceptions to the truth? There are three simple ways to start working on your blind spots.

First, ask God for clarity. Pray the prayer of Job: "Teach me what I cannot see; if I have done wrong, I will not do so again" Job 34:32.

Ask God to help you see what's true about you first then the situation and trust what he shows you.

Secondly, understand that God is going to put someone in your life, that true friend that is going to tell you what you need to hear not what you want to hear so don't get mad about the truth listen and trust it. I believe the reason Dennis and my relationship has stood the test of time is because we tell one another when we are wrong and we expect each other to correct it, as a matter of fact we hold one another accountable to fix it. Now my other children I'm still having to do a lot of work with, but Kelvin and Val are really good about getting it right when I have to get on them.

Now let me tell y'all a story about one time after me getting onto Val about something and after the conversation apparently she told Adam that I made her sick always fussing so he called to tell on her, so first I fussed at him for being a snitch then I called her to get onto her again that's because I watch her blind spot.

If you think you can work on yourself by yourself, then that in itself is a blind spot. That is self-deception. Fools think they need no advice, but the wise listen to others.

In John 14:6 the Bible says the truth will set you free. So, the closer you are to Jesus, the more your life will be filled with the truth. That means you're going to be less vulnerable to self-deception as you walk in the light of God's truth. God's truth helps you see yourself and others as you really are.

John 9:39, "I have come into the world to give sight to those who are spiritually blind and to show those who think they see that they are blind. He wasn't talking about physical blindness. He was saying, "I've come to earth to help you see your blind spots and to help you get your sight so that you can see yourself as you really are."

God can deliver you from your hidden faults, blind spots, and self-deceptions but one you have to want to be better and you have to trust him. Now I also think we sometimes need that person that questions everything now Sabrina and Cali can really make me mad sometimes because they question everything, but they also make me better.

Scripture Reference

Proverbs 12:15

Fools think their own way is right, but the wise listen to others.

34

God's Wisdom vs The World Schemes

There are too many people connected to some kind of scheme and they are only fooling themselves when they think there scheming will beat Gods wisdom, and some of these very people don't understand why they continue to struggle in life because I don't care how clever you think you are God is always do two things for sure protect his children from your schemes and reveal you in time, now this is just me. I think the worst part is when a brother or sister tries to get over on each other when I say a brother or sisters I'm referring to another Believer simply because if you know God's word then you understand that you will reap what you sow, so if you are always looking for a way to get over on people then someone will get over on you so all that scheming is really stupidity.

Now let's talk about Wisdom:

Worldly wisdom is experience, knowledge, and good judgement that make a person difficult to shock or deceive.

Godly Wisdom is the kind of wisdom that comes from the very heart of God. It's wisdom that protects and warns you against peoples deceptive ways, it is considerate and give you strength and power to not only see and reveal deception but you have them under control so that when you have the opportunity to hurt somebody you don't because you understand that in your wisdom God will prevail you and destroy them.

True wisdom only comes from God's Word, the Bible. 1 Corinthians 3:18 says, "Don't fool yourself. Don't think that you can be wise merely by being up-to-date with the latest technology or trans.

Now let's talk about the education fool for a second:

In Proverbs 14:7-9

7 Stay away from a fool, for you will not find knowledge on their lips. 8 The wisdom of the prudent is to give thought to their ways, but the folly of fools is deception.

9 Fools mock at making amends for sin, but goodwill is found among the upright.

Now these are those people that sometimes read a lot and know what God word says but they don't live it in their hearts and while they are constantly trying to make a fool out of you they are merely securing there place in hell.

Some of us confuse people that know how to be wealthy with people of wisdom. True wisdom is walking with God and to do that you need to spend time reading, studying the Bible and hearing the word of God by the person of God that has been anointed to share his messages.

I've said this before I can't tell you how many times I've prepared a sermon at night and when the congregation comes in that God changed his sermon because there a message that the congregation needed. Sometimes he would allow me to fill their spirit.

Ask God to give you a desire for his wisdom over any worldly wisdom. When you live in light of what he reveals to you in his Word, you won't need to know everything in the world. You won't need to be right all the time. You'll just want to know more of God and his love because it is the only thing that will satisfy you.

King Solomon asked for wisdom and God added the things that he needed.

Scripture Reference

1 Corithtinas 3:10-11, 18-21

According to the grace of God which is given unto me, as a wise masterbuilder, I have laid the foundation, and another buildeth thereon. But let every man take heed how he buildeth thereupon. For other foundation can no man lay than that is laid, which is Jesus Christ. Let no man deceive himself. If any man among you seemeth to be wise in this world, let him become a fool, that he may be wise. For the wisdom of this world is foolishness with God. For it is written, He taketh the wise in their own craftiness. And again, The Lord knoweth the thoughts of the wise, that they are vain. Therefore let no man glory in men. For all things are yours.

35

THE GIFT OF GENEROSITY

What is generosity?

the quality of being kind and generous.

"I was overwhelmed by the generosity of friends and neighbors."

In 2 Corinthians 9:6-8

Remember this: Whoever sows sparingly will also reap sparingly, and whoever sows generously will also reap generously. Each of you should give what you have decided in your heart to give, not reluctantly or under compulsion, for God loves a cheerful giver.

Generosity teaches us to trust God

The Bible reminds us that life on earth is uncertain and nothing is guaranteed, but when we put our hope in God's provision, we can rest assured that he'll provide for our needs.

Guys I will be completely honest here with you. I rarely preach on this subject not because of the importance of it but I was wrong because I see people suffering and don't know that when I explain to them that a large part of their struggles is because they have yet to understand that you can't beat God in giving and that when you are always waiting for God to do something in your life but you never give to the church or do anything to help anyone else then you will always live a life of lacking. One of my granddaughters is with me a lot, but my son is going to fix the problem of me not seeing the other one more I'm not asking him, I'm telling him but Cali is with me a lot and when I see people on the side of the road asking for money I do try and help, yes I know some of them really just don't need it or as we say they just want drug money or wine money but I don't help them completely for them I do it because God requires it of us. It's funny how we want to believe the Bible for everything except giving.

Before my mom left this world she taught me two very important lessons: one to completely trust God and the second one, to help people that can't help you and some of these were people that mistreated her even family but she was still there to help them and their kids she was a amazing Angel before she got to heaven. Now I think the only two times I got jealous was one when our cousin came to live with us, she loved his big head and would fix his plate before fixing mine and she kept Vince Edward for a short period of time, and when I would drop him off in the morning she had breakfast laid out for him and when I picked him up after work he would be eating a tremendous dinner, but that was her, she gave more than she received from people but God always provided for her and her unselfish prayers because rather than pray for material things she prayed for God to watch over us and I know God has done actually that.

Now let's talk about why some of us live a life of lack, it's because some of us have yet to trust God word of giving I know, I know it's hard to tithe or help someone when you don't have enough for yourself but let me ask this question before you got in the position of not having enough were you doing what God has asked of you as far as being a giver or are you still trying to make a deal with God, when my finances get better then I'm going to tithe, when I get myself together I'm going back to church, when I get where I need to be then I'm going to help someone else. Chances are you aren't going to get there and if you do it aren't going to last or you won't be happy there.

But when we learn to be more generous with God has given us, we become less selfish—more like God—and you will be given even more because he knows he can trust you to be generous with it.

Learning to trust God is a lifelong process especially with the things that we feel like we worked so hard for or things that we feel like we have little of but I just believe that when we learn the gift of giving we don't lack for anything now there's going to always be things we want that we might not get or in some cases we haven't seen yet, but I do know this for certain that when we are in the spirit and then God shows us what to pray for God always provide it.

In other words, put God first in your lives, and all of His blessings will follow. The blessings of the gospel, eternal families, spiritual strength, increased knowledge, peace in our hearts, comfort to our souls, and so many others all flow into our lives when we put God first.

Scripture Reference

Proverbs 10:22

When the LORD blesses you with riches, you have nothing to regret.

36

Do You Have What You Need?

Did you know there's a bank in heaven?

In Philippians 4:6 Paul says, "Do not be anxious about anything, but in everything by prayer and supplication with thanksgiving let your requests be made known to God."

And then in Philippians 4:19 (just 13 verses later), he gives the liberating promise of future grace: "My God will supply every need of yours according to his riches in glory in Christ Jesus."

If we live by faith in this promise of future grace, it will be very hard for anxiety to survive. God's "riches in glory" are inexhaustible. He really means for us not to worry about our future.

But here's the thing we have to stop trying to store them here on earth.

In the book of Luke talks about storing up treasure in heaven. As a Christian, this should be the bank where you make the greatest investments of our time, talent, and resources.

In the book of James, the generosity of God toward his followers is emphasized in five different places. He says everything you have is because of God's generosity. You'd have nothing if it weren't for God. You wouldn't even exist! Every good and perfect gift comes from God—it's all because of his generosity.

God's generosity with you should make you generous with other people. You should use what you've been given to also help other people. Yes, I know sometimes people make it hard to help them because of all the scam's going on but remember it's because you are doing what God wants you to do as simple as that.

Whatever you do to point people to Jesus Christ will be stored in your bank in heaven. You're making an investment in eternity when you use your resources for the most important thing: helping people have a relationship with God.

One day a very wealthy man came to Jesus and asked him how to prepare for eternity in heaven. This man had far more money than he needed or could even enjoy. He wanted to know how he could have eternal life.

Jesus instructed him to liquidate some of your assets here on earth and send them on ahead to heaven, where your treasure will last forever. Now if you have read the story the young man went away sad because. What he didn't understand is that you can't beat God's giving. When you are faithful in your tithes at church, faithful at helping others God will bring it back to you ten times more than what you gave. Now here's the problem, some people take that word and take off thinking that if they give God 10 dollars tomorrow someone will give them 100 dollars and I'm not sure that will happen, but I can tell you this every time I help a brother in need God always blesses me with more. After I tithe in church Sabrina and I are always able to have a nice after service meal together.

When you're generous in God's word it changes your perspective on how you see things and more importantly when you really learn the importance of helping others not only does it make you feel good, you are storing up treasure in heaven.

What are the five rewards that's stored in heaven for you

1 Crown of Life.

2 Incorruptible Crown.

3 Crown of Righteousness.

4 Crown of Glory.

5 Crown of Rejoicing.

SCRIPTURE REFERENCE

Luke 12:22

Sell your possessions and give to those in need. This will store up treasure for you in heaven! And the purses of heaven never get old or develop holes. Your treasure will be safe; no thief can steal it and no moth can destroy it.

37

LET YOUR TRIALS
MAKE YOU MORE LIKE JESUS

Adversity and challenges of life is something that we all must face in our lifetime and there's no way around it but we do have a choice on how we handle it, we can come unglued and take the woe is me approach our we can allow it to bring us closer to God.

James 1:3-7

3 Knowing this, that the trying of your faith worketh patience.

4 But let patience have her perfect work, that ye may be perfect and entire, wanting nothing.

5 If any of you lack wisdom, let him ask of God, that giveth to all men liberally, and upbraideth not; and it shall be given him.

6 But let him ask in faith, nothing wavering. For he that wavereth is like a wave of the sea driven with the wind and tossed.

7 For let not that man think that he shall receive any thing of the Lord.

So yes you will undoubtedly face stress, problems, difficulties, and trouble in this life. But I have some good news trouble don't last always and the more you search for God the less the things that people try and bring up in your life will affect how you approach your day. Now I know when you are going through something let's be honest it feels like forever but let me also ask you these questions have you given that problem over to God? Have you made a decision to trust God all the way to the end? Are you doing the things that required of you to be delivered from what you are going through?

Guys I can't tell you how many times God has waited on me to learn the lesson that he needed me to learn during what I thought were difficult times but what they really were times for me to learn.

My life is lived through lessons not by lacking because my God has always supplied me with everything that I need to have prosperity, happiness and joy, now don't get me wrong Satan is out there and he keeps trying to get into God's and my business now I know God isn't going to let him in it's just my job to keep him out as well.

Starting right now I need each of you that's truly reading these messages to text me individually about one thing that you are trusting God for a we are going to pray together for his deliverance about it, now I need for you to be positive about the whole situation I need you to speak positive about it every day I will do the same let's do this through this all the way until the end of this year and watch God work.

Our God is not cold, unfeeling or capricious. Rather, He is our loving heavenly Father whose heart is tender toward His children. Jesus reminds us that just as an earthly father would not deny his children bread, so God has promised to give us "good gifts" when we ask Him and one of the most important things is that he will also teach you what to ask for.

God's Promises To Satisfies Us With Long Life

With a long life I will satisfy him. –Psalm 91:16

The sixth promise—to satisfy those who love Him with a long life—is found in verse 16. God does not just say that He will prolong our lives and give us a lot of birthdays. No! He says that He will satisfy us with a long life.

Now let's talk about what a long life means with God because we can live a long time. A long life with God will not be a life that's always lacking the things that brings you comfort, peace, stability, happiness, joy and most importantly love. So let me say this and I say it out of love, if you are not experiencing these things then I need you to really listen to God when you are talking to him because we are really good at telling him what we want but we miss it when he tells us how to get there or we are not fully in, we keep straddling the fence and I can tell you for certain God will not move for us as long as we do.

It has been said that there is a God-shaped vacuum on the inside of each one of us. If we will come to Him, let Him fill that empty place on the inside, and allow Him to fulfill the call on our lives—then He will give us a long life and satisfy us as we live it out.

God wants us to live a prosperous happy and satisfied life, but are we living to have that life?

David was Israel's most valiant, daring warrior, yet he lived to be a ripe old age, "full of days," as the Old Testament authors liked to say. His life was filled with combat, high-risk situations, and impossible odds. Yet, he did not die in battle; his head went down in peace in his old age. Long life is a great concluding promise of protection.

I'm learning that we are really good at knowing what God promises are for us but here's why we keep missing the promises it's because we ain't doing what God told us or we ain't in the right place for the promise to be fulfilled spiritually, mentally, or physically.

Long life is a promise from God. Long life is a blessing from God. God wants you to have long days and an abundant life, but we must understand this fact: we are able to control our time on earth.

God wants you to have long life abundantly, and Satan wants you to have short life and peril. Why would God desire life for you and why would Satan desire death?

God has a plan for you. He has things He wants you to do for Him and for His kingdom. He wants you to live your life in such a way that others will be attracted to your lifestyle and desire to be like you. His desire for those who follow Him is prosperity, peace and abundance in all areas.

Now the devil, on the other hand, wants your life shortened. He knows that one Spirit-filled Christian, walking in the fullness of God, can deal a severe blow to his kingdom.

He knows that a believer who lives a long life of prosperity and health will attract others to the Kingdom of God. Satan hates God and will do everything possible to make the Kingdom of God look unappealing. Satan is the king of deception. He tempts us and tricks us into missing God's blessing of long life by tempting us into disobedience.

Here's the things I need you all the know the only power that Satan has is the power that we give him but if God is for us who can be against us, we have a decision to make

Scripture Reference

In Psalm 91:16
With long life I will satisfy him and show him my salvation.

Deuteronomy 5:33
You shall walk in all the way that the Lord your God has commanded you, that you may live, and that it may go well with you, and that you may live long in the land that you shall possess.

Proverbs 16:31
Gray hair is a crown of glory; it is gained in a righteous life.

1 Peter 3:10
For "Whoever desires to love life and see good days, let him keep his tongue from evil and his lips from speaking deceit.

_____
_____
_____
_____

38

GOD HONORS ME

...I will honor him... –Psalm 91:15

The fifth promise—to honor those who love God—is in the last part of verse fifteen.

What does it really mean to say that God honors me? When God bestows His honor upon you, you enjoy "distinguished respect and dignity". Life is worthless without divine honor. Too many times we look for or want honor from man but that same man that honor you one moment will curse you the next so me personally I don't need man's honor, but when God honors you, your life will be meaningful, protected and blessed.

It is truly a mind-boggling concept to think that God would tell us that He would honor us. Let's think about what it looks like when God places His honor on someone's life. Have you had a time when you have been favored by God? Interestingly, it can be challenging for a period of time. Why would God tell Joseph in a dream about the coming honor He would give him?

When Joseph told his father and brothers Please listen to this dream which I have had; for behold, we were binding sheaves in the field, and lo, my sheaf rose up and also stood erect; and behold, your sheaves gathered around and bowed down to my sheaf... Lo, I have had still another dream; and behold, the sun and the moon and eleven stars were bowing down to me." Genesis 36:6-7, 9

Seems like after Joseph told them the dream all hell broke loose he was sold to slavery, his masters wife tried to rape him then accused him of trying to rape her, thrown in prison for a crime he didn't commit but the most amazing thing happened in those events in his life, it prepared him for his purpose with God, it gave him honor with God and he fulfilled his purpose for God and he was honored by the very people that wanted to cause him harm.

Now Joseph could have become bitter and set out to get revenge on everyone that caused him harm but instead he chose love and I just believe that's the best honor we can have because if God honors us that means blessings follows, growth follows, promotions follow and peace follows us.

Honor is a unique gift God gives us and that honor also extends to our family as well and he honors us just because he loves us.

1 Samuel 2:30

Therefore the LORD, the God of Israel, declares: 'I promised that members of your family would minister before me forever. ' But now the LORD declares: 'Far be it from me! Those who honor me I will honor, but those who despise me will be disdained.

Proverbs 22:4

Humility is the fear of the LORD; its wages are riches and honor and life. God Rescues Me From Trouble

…I will be with him in trouble; I will rescue him… –Psalm 91:15

The fourth promise—to rescue from trouble those who love the Lord—is found in the middle of verse 15. It is a well-known fact that human nature cries out to God when faced with trouble. We've all known people in crisis call out to God and yes there's been a lot of people that criticize people that only seek God during the difficult times but what I always try and explain to people what better time than when you are faced with difficulties than the seek God, my prayers are for you to always seek him, during trouble or good times. What I've found in my search for God is that he keeps me grounded in good times and lifts me up during the bad. See God protects us even when we don't see trouble coming so I know that he protects when we are seeking him, for me the things that I've found out that works in my life is that when I continue to seek him I'm able to remain in his presence which helps me in every phase of my life.

To be honest If a person has never felt danger or gone through difficulties then some of them would have never turned to God in the first place but let me tell you something they are welcomed in the house of God and those holier than thou people had better hope they have a seat in the kingdom.

God answers our prayers and rescues us in so many ways. I am so thankful that He is creative and not limited by our seemingly impossible situations. But we have to ask in faith and not confine Him to our limited resources. God says, "If you love Me, I will be with you when you find yourself in trouble, and I will rescue you." But we have to trust Him to do it His way.

Whether or not we can experience or sense God, He is always there with during every step of our journey with him especially in our troubled times. His presence is an objective fact, even in times when we can't feel Him. This is why we pray, stay in the Word and seek the Holy Spirit. This reality supports and empowers us to continue to move towards him.

SCRIPTURE REFERENCE

Isaiah 43:2-3

When you pass through the waters, I will be with you; And through the rivers, they shall not overflow you. When you walk through the fire, you shall not be burned, Nor shall the flame scorch you. For I am the Lord your God, The Holy One of Israel, your Savior; I gave Egypt for your ransom, Ethiopia and Seba in your place."

_____
_____
_____
_____
_____
_____
_____

39

GOD ANSWERS MY CALL

He will call on Me, and I will answer him… –Psalm 91:15

God makes a third promise here in verse fifteen that He will answer those who truly love Him and call on His Name. Are we aware of what a wonderful promise God is making to us?

Nothing gives me more comfort than to realize that every time I pray in line with God's Word, He hears me. And, if He hears me, I know I have the request for which I asked. This is one of the promises that keeps me continually searching His Word in order to understand His will and His promises so that I can know how to have a more effective prayer life and relationship with God. Now let me see if I can bring clarity to what Moses is explaining here, the more we search for God in the spirit, the more we want what God wants for us and our prayers fall in line with his will for us and his love for us increases our faith which allows us to be constant in his presence which keeps us in his perfect peace, blessings, protection, deliverance and love and guys I can tell you there's no greater love than the love that God has shown us.

Now I understand that this is still difficult for some of us that's why we still struggle with anger, depression at times, uncertainty at times but the more we trust God with everything the less we struggle with the other things, we need to be to a point where we depend on him solely for EVERYTHING.

When our hearts calls out to Him, He hears our call. We are not calling out to a God who isn't there or who is blind or deaf to our needs. We are calling to a God that not only created us but who also loves us and his desired for us is to have prosperity, peace, abundant blessings, and his special love which is why he created us and has every intention of us being in Heaven with him.

SCRIPTURE REFERENCE

I John 5:14-15

This is the confidence we have before Him, that, if we ask anything according to His will, He hears us. And if we know that He hears us in whatever we ask, we know that we have the requests which we have asked from Him.

_____
_____
_____
_____
_____
_____
_____

40

I Am Seated With Him On High

To be set securely on high is the second promise to those who love the Lord and know Him by Name. When God wants to show something important about Himself or about His promises in the Old Testament, He would make it known by revealing another one of His covenant Names. His Name revealed Himself: Jehovah Jireh is above lack, Jehovah Rapha is higher than sickness, and Jehovah Shalom is above a restless mind. And it's so important that we understand that he's the same God today.

His Name above all other names also in Ephesians 1:20-21; 2:6 ...which He brought about in Christ, when He raised Him from the dead, and seated Him at His right hand in the heavenly places, far above all rule and authority and power and dominion and every name that is named, not only in this age, but also in the one to come... and raised us up with Him, and seated us with Him in the heavenly places, in Christ Jesus.

God pulls us up to where He is? Let me say that again God pulls us up to where he is! Our vantage point is greatly improved when we are seated with Him on high.

Notice that this verse Psalm 91:14, uses the word "known." Do you know Him by Name? These promises come out of having a known relationship with Him.

In order to receive his blessing's, his promises, his protection, his deliverance and his love you have to have a personal relationship with him that means studying your Bible, going to church, having a active prayer life and obeying his word. These are the things that connects us to him and all of his promises to us.

In the first two sentences of Psalm 91, the Moses refers to God by four different names. God is The Most High, revealing that He is the highest that exists. God is called The Almighty, denoting that He is the most powerful. He is referred to as The Lord, revealing ownership. Then Moses calls Him My God, making it personal. This promise of being seated securely on high is reserved for the one who experiences God intimately, then God says that the promises are ours.

To be seated High from a Believers perspective, the idea of sitting in heavenly places is challenging to grasp, especially on this side of eternity. Nevertheless, this is the experience of everyone who is redeemed by God's grace: "But God, being rich in mercy, because of the great love with which he loved us, even when we were dead in our trespasses, made us alive together with Christ—by grace you have been saved—and raised us up with him and seated us with him in the heavenly places in Christ Jesus, so that in the coming ages he might show the immeasurable riches of his grace in kindness toward us in Christ Jesus.

Scripture Reference

Psalms 91:14

Because he has loved Me... I will set him securely on high because he has known My Name.

41

GOD IS MY DELIVERER

Psalms 91:1-16

91 He that dwelleth in the secret place of the most High shall abide under the shadow of the Almighty.

2 I will say of the Lord, He is my refuge and my fortress: my God; in him will I trust.

3 Surely he shall deliver thee from the snare of the fowler, and from the noisome pestilence.

4 He shall cover thee with his feathers, and under his wings shalt thou trust: his truth shall be thy shield and buckler.

5 Thou shalt not be afraid for the terror by night; nor for the arrow that flieth by day;

6 Nor for the pestilence that walketh in darkness; nor for the destruction that wasteth at noonday.

7 A thousand shall fall at thy side, and ten thousand at thy right hand; but it shall not come nigh thee.

8 Only with thine eyes shalt thou behold and see the reward of the wicked.

9 Because thou hast made the Lord, which is my refuge, even the most High, thy habitation;

10 There shall no evil befall thee, neither shall any plague come nigh thy dwelling.

11 For he shall give his angels charge over thee, to keep thee in all thy ways.

12 They shall bear thee up in their hands, lest thou dash thy foot against a stone.

13 Thou shalt tread upon the lion and adder: the young lion and the dragon shalt thou trample under feet.

14 Because he hath set his love upon me, therefore will I deliver him: I will set him on high, because he hath known my name.

15 He shall call upon me, and I will answer him: I will be with him in trouble; I will deliver him, and honour him.

16 With long life will I satisfy him, and shew him my salvation.

Psalm 91 is God's promise to us of deliverance, it's one the first of the seven promises made to the one who loves God.

Each Believer should take this personal Make it personal, it's because of his love I can face tomorrow, because of his love I know that no weapon formed against me shall prosper.

Guys I would never tell you that when you love God, trust God, seek God, and seek God's obedience in your life that everything will just fall in place and you will not have situations or circumstances going on in your life but honestly I think that the more you love and seek God, the Satan will attack you but I will tell you this the more you trust him the less effect of the foolishness that Satan does will effect or bother you and the more you will realize Gods love for you.

Joel 2:32

All who call on the Name of the Lord shall be delivered.

Let me say this we all of desperately need God's promise of deliverance but not all of us will seek it and some of us still don't understand the power we possess as God's children.

There are also other types of deliverances. There is the internal and the external. Ask yourself, "From what is He going to deliver me?"

God will deliver us from all of the following:

- Lion problems (life-threatening attacks)

- Young lion problems (constant harassment)

- Cobra problems (sneaky attacks which seem to come out of nowhere)

- Dragon problems (imaginary fears, past fears, vain imaginations)

- Terror by night (evils that come through man—war, terror, violence)

- Arrows that fly by day (enemy assignments sent to wound)

- Pestilence (plagues, deadly diseases, fatal epidemics)

- Destruction (evils over which man has no control)

God has every intention of delivering us from any and all kinds of evil rather it's Spiritual or earthly things that we need delivering from.

Scripture Reference

Psalms 32:7

You are my hiding place; You shall preserve me from trouble; You shall surround me with songs of deliverance.

Luke 1:37

For with God nothing will be impossible.

We Do Not Have To Fear Destruction

You will not be afraid of the destruction that lays waste at noon. –Psalm 91:6-7

6 Nor for the pestilence that walketh in darkness; nor for the destruction that wasteth at noonday.

7 A thousand shall fall at thy side, and ten thousand at thy right hand; but it shall not come nigh thee.

The fourth category of evil is destruction. Destruction takes in the evils which mankind has no control—those things that the world ignorantly calls acts of God: tornadoes, floods, hurricanes, fire. But if God clearly tells us that we are not to fear destruction. Then how can these so-called natural disasters be coming from God?

As Believers there's so much that we need to learn about God and so much that we need to ignore of what man says or should I say assumes.

In Mark 4:39, Jesus rebuked the storm, and it became perfectly calm, demonstrating that God is not the author of such things. Otherwise, Jesus would never have contradicted His Father by rebuking something sent by Him and as Believers we need to know that God is about building not destroying.

Now I realize that there's is no place in the physical world where you can go and be safe from every destruction—every natural disaster. We can never anticipate what might come when we least expect it, but no matter where you are in this world, God says to run to His shelter where you will not be afraid of the destruction…it will not approach you!

God lets us know in Psalm 91, "You will not be afraid of terror, arrows, pestilence or destruction because I have said in My Word that it will not approach you—if you are obedient to verses one and two to dwell in My shelter and abide in My shadow." And, of course, we cannot dwell and abide in Him apart from Jesus, but, praise God—because of the shed Blood of the Cross, it has now been made possible. Guys you can tell Satan just like MC Hammer said Can't Touch This!

This is important we are able to receive and have anything that God has already provided. The secret is knowing that everything for which God has made provision is clearly spelled out and defined in the Word of God and we can have it if we ask and believe what we ask for, If you can find where God has offered it—you can have it! It is never God holding it back. His provision is already there waiting to be received but we have to continuously seek Him.

Faith is the means by which we accept what God has already made available. Our goal needs to be the renewal of our minds, so we have more faith, more obedience, more trust and a true hunger for God and his word. Guys I can tell you this for sure God is getting ready to do something, something that is going to affect a lot of people lives for the better, now not everyone is going to receive this blessing because some are not capable of seeking him in love and truth.

SCRIPTURE REFERENCE

Mark 4:37-41

37 And there arose a great storm of wind, and the waves beat into the ship, so that it was now full.

38 And he was in the hinder part of the ship, asleep on a pillow: and they awake him, and say unto him, Master, carest thou not that we perish?

39 And he arose, and rebuked the wind, and said unto the sea, Peace, be still. And the wind ceased, and there was a great calm.

40 And he said unto them, Why are ye so fearful? how is it that ye have no faith?

41 And they feared exceedingly, and said one to another, What manner of man is this, that even the wind and the sea obey him?

43

WE DO NOT HAVE TO FEAR THE PANDEMIC OR OTHER PESTILENCE

When fighting the fears of fatal diseases, these are the Scripture for us to take hold of!

The third category of evil that God names is pestilence. This is the only evil He names twice. Since God doesn't waste words, He must have a specific reason for repeating this promise. God knew the pestilence and the fear that would be running rampant in these end days. The world is teeming with fatal epidemics that are hitting people by the thousands, so God catches our attention by repeating this promise.

It's as though God is saying, "I said it in verse three, but did you really hear Me? Just to be sure, I am saying it again in verse six—you do not have to be afraid of the deadly pestilence!" This is so necessary for the world we live in today but I also think it also includes all the killings that going on around us in our neighborhoods, churches and schools. We have to renew our thinking before we can comprehend the fact that we do not have to be afraid of the sicknesses, diseases and all of this hate that are epidemic in the world today.

Our inheritance is not limited to what is handed down to us genetically from our ancestors. Our inheritance is because of what Jesus did on the cross for us, what he did was buy our safety, our deliverance and our peace of mind with his very body as a sacrifice. Now that doesn't mean that things will not come up but what means is no weapon formed against us shall prosper but we have to believe that we will be rewarded when we seek him.

Let me see if I can explain why it's so important to understand what really happened we Jesus died in the Cross, Jesus, God's Son, came to earth to reunite us with God through the ultimate sacrifice: his own life. We could never a life worthy of God on our own. So Jesus lived a life without sin on our behalf. And then he died the painful death our sins deserve.

When he died on the Cross two things happened

1. Jesus Died to Bring Us Near to God, Christ died for sins once for all, the righteous for the unrighteous, to bring you to God. (1 Pet. 3:18)

2. Jesus Died to Reveal God's Character, His providential care for creation reveals his love. And his promises to Abraham show his concern for the whole world. But at the cross, we see the climax of his covenants with Israel, and we witness the final and dramatic proof of his love and justice for all of us that confess with our mouths and believe in our hearts that he is who he says he is.

Scripture Reference

Psalms 91:3

Surely he shall deliver thee from the snare of the fowler, and from the noisome pestilence.

Psalms 91:6

You will not be afraid of the pestilence that stalks in darkness.

44

I Will Not Fear The Arrow

You will not be afraid of the... arrow that flies by day. –Psalm 91:5

The word arrow is not to be found in the New Testament. In the Old Testament it is used repeatedly, especially in the Psalms. It comes from the root Hebrew word which means to divide, to cut into two parts; then that which cuts in two, divides, wounds, destroys; and finally, an arrow with its cutting head.

The second category of evil is the arrow that flies by day. An arrow is something that pierces or wounds spiritually, physically, mentally, or emotionally. This category indicates that you are in a spiritual battle zone—specific enemy assignments directed toward your life to defeat you.

Arrows are deliberately sent by the enemy and meticulously aimed at the spot that will cause the most damage. They are targeted toward the area where our mind where we are weak, you know that area where you still haven't been able to control you know what I mean that area where we are still losing our temper, still get easily offended, area of rebellion, still trying to live Godly and worldly at the same time, you know what I'm talking about that area in your life where you afraid to turn completely over to God because you won't have control well I got some bad news and some good news. Bad news first you never were in control, now Good news either is Satan.

Now this is important seldomly does Satan ever attack us in an area where we are built up and strong. He attacks us where we're still struggling and sometimes those are in the very area where we assume we are strong until he attacks but you can rest assured that he's going to attack.

That's why we must continue to stay in the presence of God and continually seeking him. When we do battle using our spiritual weapons, Satan arrows will not approach us.

I remember the one day surgery that almost killed me but instead empowered me. Satan had plans to destroy me but God's had plans way before Satan plans to lift me up to a higher level, God always win that's why I'm his child we win, I never will forget the look on Marcus and Edward's face seeing me in what appeared to be a weak point in my life, Marcus told me that it was difficult seeing me like that, that I was there Superman, now I didn't tell them this at the time but Superman wore tights and a cape leading building, I wear polo and coach defeating Satan, Superman would only be a cook in my outfit!

God tells us in Ephesians 6:12 that we have a "shield of faith to extinguish all the flaming darts of the enemy." These are not just plain arrows, they are "on fire." And God doesn't say we can miss most of them but instead He says that we can extinguish "all" of them. When arrows are sent to wound us spiritually, physically, emotionally, or financially, God wants us to ask Him and believe Him by faith that He will pick us up out of harm's way and deliver us from all calamity.

We have a promise from God telling us not to be afraid of the arrow that flies by day. That no weapon formed against us shall prosper. Now that doesn't mean that Satan will stop trying but the good news is that wherever he attacks God will use that very area where you were weak to make you strong.

Assignments will rise up, but don't be afraid. He has promised to protect us, and He has promised the arrows will not hit their target.

Let me see if I can connect all of this like this: I have a couple of young men that I'm training in basketball and weightlifting. Right now, we spend more time in the weight room than we do on the basketball court. Although they are basketball players, they need to be strengthened in some of their physical strengths to enhance their basketball gifts, but now I have to be careful not to totally focus on their physical strengths and ignore their basketball skills or I'm going to have a bunch of weightlifters and not basketball players. Old basketball metaphor: strengthen your weakness and maintain your strengths.

Scripture Reference

Ephesians 6:12
For we wrestle not against flesh and blood, but against principalities, against powers, against the rulers of the darkness of this world, against spiritual wickedness in high places.

45

THE PROTECTION OF GOD

Psalms 91:4-7

4 He shall cover thee with his feathers, and under his wings shalt thou trust: his truth shall be thy shield and buckler.

5 Thou shalt not be afraid for the terror by night; nor for the arrow that flieth by day;

6 Nor for the pestilence that walketh in darkness; nor for the destruction that wasteth at noonday.

7 A thousand shall fall at thy side, and ten thousand at thy right hand; but it shall not come nigh thee.

You are protected versus 5 and 6 covers an entire 24-hour period emphasizing day and night protection. What is more important is that these two verses encompass every evil known to man.

The psalmist divides the list into four categories. The first terror by night—includes all the evils that come through man: kidnapping, robbery, rape, murder, terrorism, wars...! It is the dread—or horror—or alarm that comes from what man can do to you. God is saying, "You will not be afraid of any of those things...because they will not approach you" (Psalm 91:5-7). The first thing verse five deals with is fear.

Now let's talk about fear for a second what is fear, it's an unpleasant emotion caused by the belief that someone or something is dangerous, cause you pain, or a threat to your life. The Bible tells us 365 times to "fear not" that's one for every day of the year. So why does the Bible tells us to "fear not" no it's not because y'all can do like Clint does. He's the President of our Company and yes like that little brother to me. He will get smart with someone and look for me to get behind afterwards but the reason the Bible tells us to fear not is because God wants us to be filled with hope and trust, not fear. He has given us hope through the promise that he can uphold us by his strength today, and he has also promised those who have faith in Jesus Christ for their salvation a life of eternity with him. Guys I have found out that there's so much more peace and happiness when we walk around without fear or worry now understand it's not because I got it all together, but it's because God has it although and he's gone ahead of me and destroyed all the enemies on my path that I have to travel to him, now mine you sometimes I try to get off the path sometimes you know how we get to look over there and want to kick the bobo with ya boy, but you know it ain't where God told you to be so sometimes he has to hit me upside the head, let me stop lying he's constantly hitting me on the head about my temper but we have this understanding he knows I love him more than anything but sometimes when people get wrong he has to remind me he got this but as far as fear now sometimes Satan will try and hit you with something that he wants you to fear but God has delivered me, saves me, protects me, and puts me back on my path in his journey.

For me, so many times Satan knows I'm going to tell him to get behind and I don't walk around in fear but instead in faith and guys I can tell you that walking around in faith looks good on me! Just asking Marcus if you don't believe me.

I need someone to not only read this next paragraph but listen to it, the goodness of God is that He made provision before we ever asked! This is not for everyone; it is for those who know and truly believe the truth. Over and over, Jesus told us, "Do not fear!" Why do you think He continually reminds us not to be afraid? Because it is through faith in His Word that we are protected—and since fear is the opposite of faith, the Lord knows fear will keep us from operating in the faith that is necessary to receive. It is no wonder God addresses the fear of terror first.

Now let's get what we came for. Do you know how to keep from being afraid? Very simply! Fear comes when we think we are responsible for bringing about this protection ourselves, you know what I'm talking about when we think we are in control or unfortunately when some of us think Satan is in control.

Too often, we think— "Oh, if I can just believe hard enough, maybe I'll be protected!" That is the wrong thinking and the farthest thing from the truth. The protection is already there. It has already been provided, whether we receive it or not. Faith is simply the choice to receive what Jesus has already done, he died on the cross for our protection and went to hell stripping Satan of any power he thought he had and on that third day when he left hell, he took the keys with him because one of these days he's going to lock Satan and all his believers in there for eternity, and y'all know misery loves company and Satan knows his time is short so let me ask you guys a question because I got this figured out: That old boy got thrown out of heaven, stripped of his title, live in a place where he don't have the keys, still have to ask for permission to mess with us has absolutely no power, unless we give it to him. So, tell me again why we're walking around in fear?

Let me tell you why we waking around trying to fight a Spiritual Battle with Our physical weapons. Now Kelvin and I have some fast hands but they ain't that fast and yes Chris would fight all day but until we start fighting this fight that we are constantly in using our Spiritual weapons we will continue to walk around defeated in FEAR!

See operating in the Spirit consist of us operating in our spiritual weapons with our mouths and hearts. Confessing with our mouth and believing with our heart starts with the new birth experience and sets precedence for receiving all of God's good gifts (Romans 10:9-10).

With true faith, we can walk confidently into the future knowing that God is able to hold us, sustain us, empower us, heal us, and strengthen us, no matter what. Because He has done it before, and He is the same yesterday, today, and forever

Scripture Reference

Hebrews 13:6-8

6 So that we may boldly say, The Lord is my helper, and I will not fear what man shall do unto me.

7 Remember them which have the rule over you, who have spoken unto you the word of God: whose faith follow, considering the end of their conversation.

8 Jesus Christ the same yesterday, and today, and forever.

THE SHIELD OF GOD

Shield means to protect (someone or something) from a danger, risk, or unpleasant. To have the strong assurance in the person and work of Jesus Christ that you are his, you belong to him, you fight under his shield and he protects you as his own.

It is God's faithfulness to His promises that is our shield. It is not just our faithfulness! God will be faithful to the promises He has made. Even when the enemy comes to whisper fearful or condemning thoughts in our mind, we can ward off his attack by saying, "My faith is strong because I know My God is faithful, and His faithfulness is my shield!"

I think the biggest mistake we make as Believers is to think, "I can't dwell in the shelter of God. I mess up and fall short too many times. I feel guilty and unworthy." God knows all about our weaknesses that no matter how much we try we could never earn salvation it's free because of what Jesus did for us on the cross. Think about it if we were prefect can could handle this on our own we won't need Jesus.

The main thing is—if we slip and fall, we must not stay down. Get up, repent, and get back under that shield of protection. Thankfully this verse says it is His faithfulness, not ours, that is our shield. Again, it's okay to fall, to fail but what's not ok is to remain in foolishness or just accept missing the mark, he didn't choose. you because he thought you were perfect but instead, he chose in spite of your lack of perfection. You are that warrior that refuses to stand down in sin, mistakes and doubts.

Too many of us are still focused on where we were instead of where God is taking me, too many of us can still hear people that doubted us instead of listening to God's encouragement, and some of us haven't realized that we are more than conquerors. We have been told to go forth in search of where God wants to bless us and we keep assuming we have to tackle these Giants when God has already told us that we will inhabit the land.

We dwell in His shelter by faith in God's grace (Ephesians 2:8-9). Faith is not hard. It is simply our response to what Jesus has already provided through His Blood. We cannot perform enough good deeds to keep ourselves in His shelter any more than we can do enough to keep ourselves saved. We have to realize we dwell in His shelter, not in our own righteousness, but in his righteousness and his love for us.

Scripture Reference

Psalm 91:4

His faithfulness is a shield and bulwark.

47

Protection Under His Wings

We know that in Isaiah 40:31, it talks about being borne up on the wings of eagles or with wings like eagles. But guys there's a difference, however, between being "on" His wings and being "under" His wings. This promise in Psalm 91:4 is not elaborating on the flying wing—but on the sheltering wing. One indicates strength and accomplishment, while the other indicates God's protection from the difficult things that try to harm us.

When I picture myself under the warmth of a nest and the security of being under the wings of the nurturing of God's love, I can't help but to feel his love, his strength, his blessings and it makes me want to continue to be in his presence for all these things.

The concept of taking a person "under one's wing" is familiar to us today. When an individual is alone, in a new position, or needing special guidance, another, more experienced person may offer to take the other "under his wing" to care for, teach, and guide. But in Psalm 91:4 under His wings is a metaphor for the protective refuge of God's presence. The imagery alludes to a mother bird taking her vulnerable hatchlings under her wings to nurture, train, shelter, guide, and protect.

Oh, Jerusalem, Jerusalem... How often I wanted to gather your children together, the way a hen gathers her chicks under her wings, and you were unwilling. –Matthew 23:37

But is not everyone is protected under the wings? Did you notice it says, He will cover you with His pinions (feathers), and under His wings, you may seek refuge, but so many of us don't make that decision to come to him, we keep seeking the warmth of satisfaction, protection and deliverance in things and unfortunately people that if you ain't careful we have you so mess up that you don't think that you can make it back to God but here's a simple truth that all Believers need to believe and understand if we seek him you will find protection under his wings but he will not make us , it's our decision to make.

We can seek refuge under His wings if we choose to or continue to do the things that we have been doing that doesn't protect us. See somebody has got to stop trying to find protection, guidance, love, blessings, and joy under the wings of things and people that have left us unprotected, not love, barely making and very little peace or joy in our lives. Now some people and some situations are not only necessary but they also help us to get to his protection, his love, his guidance, his peace and his blessings but not everybody is a part of God's plan for your life and those are the ones that he's trying to protect you from so you can't take them with you under the wings of his protection and that's why some of us walking around lacking is because we keep trying to hold on to foolishness and trying to fit under his wings and it ain't going to happen so you need to make a decision to turn all that stuff loose to get under his wings or stay out there miserable and lost.

Notice the contrast between His willingness and our unwillingness—His wanting to against our not willing to—His would against our would not. What an amazing analogy to show us theologically that there is protection offered that some of us will not accept and believe it or not the very ones that guilty of not accepting his protection are the ones that's the loudest in asking continuously for his protection but ain't ready to turn some things loose.

God is deeply committed to us—yet, at the same time, we can reject His outstretched arms if we so choose which unfortunately so many of us do or we can trust him and take refuge under his wings the choice is ours to make.

Scripture Reference

Isaiah 40:27-31

Why sayest thou, O Jacob, and speakest, O Israel, My way is hid from the LORD, and my judgment is passed over from my God? Hast thou not known? hast thou not heard, that the everlasting God, the LORD, the Creator of the ends of the earth, fainteth not, neither is weary? there is no searching of his understanding. He giveth power to the faint; and to them that have no might he increaseth strength. Even the youths shall faint and be weary, and the young men shall utterly fall: but they that wait upon the LORD shall renew their strength; they shall mount up with wings as eagles; they shall run, and not be weary; and they shall walk, and not faint.

48

My Deliverance

Too many times we become more focused on The Trapper and the Trap that the one that's able to protect us from all traps that Satan put out for us and you can rest assure the closer you become in your relationship with God, Satan is upset. Now let me see if I can really explain this, see the closer you become to God in your relationship with God the closer you become in securing your place in Heaven with God the very place that Satan tried to take over the very place that he got kicked out of!

But the problem is that we are still allowing Satan to have a seat in our house, on our jobs, in our relationship with other and with our health. when we don't have too.

But that doesn't mean he will not try see our enemy the Devil knows exactly what will most likely hook us, and he knows exactly which thought to put into our minds to lure us into the trap. That is why Paul tells us in 2 Corinthians 2:11 that we are "...not to be ignorant of the schemes (traps) of the enemy."

But God not only delivers us from the snare laid by Satan but He also delivers us from the deadly pestilence. Webster's New World Dictionary says pestilence is "any virulent or fatal disease; an epidemic that hits the masses of people—any deadly disease that attaches itself to one's body with the intent to destroy." But God says, "I will deliver you from the deadly disease that comes with the intent to destroy."

There are all kinds of enemies, or should I Satan has several traps up his sleeves and believe me of these few truths he will never come at you with in your strengths but instead in your weaknesses like physical and spiritual temptations or weaknesses. If you will listen to Satan long enough, he will convince you that the wrong that God has warned you about is actually God being against you, just ask Eve when you see her, see Satan is a coward he won't face you while God is with you so if you really want to defeat Satan stay connected to God. You remember when you were going places with mama and she either held your hand or you held on to her clothes? Vince Edward and I should we both held on to my mama dress following her around the house as kids, I did it and almost 38 years later so did Edward we knew as long as we stayed connected to mama everything was going to be everything.

And sometimes we just have to let Satan know who our Daddy is and what he's capable of but if we don't ever open our Bibles to know what he said then how can we let Satan to know that we rebuke him and tell him to get the behind me that I don't just live by bread alone that I need God's word daily, that I am more than a conqueror, that I can do all things in Christ Jesus.

Now let me end this like this we must learn to fight Satan not in the physical but in the spiritual.

Scripture Reference

Ephesian 6:11-14

11 Put on the full armor of God, so that you can take your stand against the devil's schemes.

12 For our struggle is not against flesh and blood, but against the rulers, against the authorities, against the powers of this dark world and against the spiritual forces of evil in the heavenly realms.

13 Therefore put on the full armor of God, so that when the day of evil comes, you may be able to stand your ground, and after you have done everything, to stand.

14 Stand firm then, with the belt of truth buckled around your waist, with the breastplate of righteousness in place.

_____
_____
_____
_____
_____
_____
_____
_____
_____
_____
_____

49

DWELLING PLACE IN MY SECRET PLACE

Guys we are in the beginning of a new series. For the next couple of days we are going to talk about dwelling in our secret place.

When Moses wrote Psalms 91

He reminds us we are not alone, even in the midst of problems or challenge, he will not let us alone. Moses reminds us of God protection, especially during our times of hardship; when life is draining and there seems to be no time or place to rest. This book of Psalm is reassuring, comforting and encouraging, it's a call remain confidence in God and so is a call away from the cynicism of our age. At a time when many people seem to live only for the moment (because beyond that, who knows what will happen), Psalm 91 is a call to confidence in a God who, when we make him our resting place, he will never leave us alone.

Have you ever been in a place where on the outside all hell was breaking loose but you were at peace on the inside. I'm not talking about a building, a house or place but when things around you have broken out in a full range of hell on the outside you know what I'm talking about like when the pandemic hit us, and everybody was panicking and just knew it was end of the world. I remember it because I got a phone call while I was at home with Covid telling me that I needed to figure out how we were going to survive at work when our livelihood depended on how we made school furniture because we produced it with three and four people working close together. So, while I was at home and my wife making me sleep in the back bedroom where she would bring my food upstairs knock on the door after putting it on wood standing tray and run downstairs before I could make it to the door, everyone else was living in a pandemic. I was living in my dwelling place. See they saw chaos but I saw me getting all my meals brought to me, I had a chance to watch the series Merlin all night and sleep all day without someone asking me to take out the trash, clean up behind yourself, and oh yeah did I tell that you God gave me the vision on how to build a table that my guys at work could work on individually. The tables would increase our production by a third and we started getting more orders because other companies had to close because they didn't have a way to produce furniture without having multiple people on one table. See most people were in a pandemic, but I was in my dwelling place with God.

Did you know there is a place in God, a secret place, for those who want to seek refuge? It is a literal place of physical safety and security. In verse one, God is offering us more than protection; it's as if He personally invites us in to dwell with Him.

Now I need someone to think about what it means when God invite you to dwell with him?

First what actually is dwelling with God? means I am aware of who he is not the stuff that's happening around me that I'm constantly aware of what he capable of at all times and I know who he is and what he has done for me and what he will do for me. I talk with him constantly throughout my day and my focus is on him.

Our Heavenly Father has a Secret Place in His arms that protects us from the storms raging in the world around us. That Secret Place is literal, but it is also conditional! In verse one, God lists our part of the condition before He mentions the promises included in His part. That's because our part must come first. In order to abide in the shadow of the Almighty, we must choose to dwell in the shelter of the Most High. God will never force us to come to him but the most amazing thing is he waiting for YOU.

You might call that place of refuge—a Love Walk! It's a place where you will find the most important relationship of your life, it's a place where you find love like no other, it's a place where you know that you are fully protected. It's a place of great intimacy and investment of time with God that not only will he heal, protect and guide you but it's a place if development and rest.

SCRIPTURE REFERENCE

Psalms 91:1-16

1 He that dwelleth in the secret place of the most High shall abide under the shadow of the Almighty.

2 I will say of the Lord, He is my refuge and my fortress: my God; in him will I trust.

3 Surely he shall deliver thee from the snare of the fowler, and from the noisome pestilence.

4 He shall cover thee with his feathers, and under his wings shalt thou trust: his truth shall be thy shield and buckler.

5 Thou shalt not be afraid for the terror by night; nor for the arrow that flieth by day;

6 Nor for the pestilence that walketh in darkness; nor for the destruction that wasteth at noonday.

7 A thousand shall fall at thy side, and ten thousand at thy right hand; but it shall not come nigh thee.

8 Only with thine eyes shalt thou behold and see the reward of the wicked.

9 Because thou hast made the Lord, which is my refuge, even the most High, thy habitation;

10 There shall no evil befall thee, neither shall any plague come nigh thy dwelling.

11 For he shall give his angels charge over thee, to keep thee in all thy ways.

12 They shall bear thee up in their hands, lest thou dash thy foot against a stone.

13 Thou shalt tread upon the lion and adder: the young lion and the dragon shalt thou trample under feet.

14 Because he hath set his love upon me, therefore will I deliver him: I will set him on high, because he hath known my name.

15 He shall call upon me, and I will answer him: I will be with him in trouble; I will deliver him, and honour him.

16 With long life will I satisfy him, and shew him my salvation.

50

DRAWING NEAR TO GOD

What does it mean to draw near to God?

To seek after God with our whole hearts. This is what prayer and fasting is all about. We are not on a hunger strike thinking we can force God to do something. But we have purifying ourselves and removing anything that can get in way of inviting God in the midst of what we have to deal with. When we seek God and humble yourself ourselves through prayer and fasting for God to transform us and position us to walk in His perfect will. We remove the impediments that block our prayers from reaching the ears of God. It is about seeking God with everything in us.

In James 4:1-10

talks all about pride and submission. It calls for us to submit to God in order to draw nearer to Him and all the benefits of being submissive to God and all the things he is going to bless us with.

In 2 Chronicles 15:1-2, we see the Spirit of God communicate with Azariah, the son of Obed. It tells Azariah that if he seeks Him and the things of God, God will be with him. But if Azariah forsakes Him and doesn't draw near to God and he's forsaken. Nothing good comes from be pridefully instead of drawing near to God.

When our hearts are polluted with pride, lust, and deceit we develop a hardness of things from away from the things of God. To draw near to God, we must purify ourselves (empty me of me), obey truth through the power of the Holy Spirit, and fervently and sincerely love with a pure heart.

I continue to witness to a couple of you that God is getting ready to do something he has been waking me up every morning round 3:00 and eventually he will reveal to me why, now there has been times he would do that to warn me about evil now let me state this before we go farther with the message, some of us become fearful when God wakes us to warn us but I want you all to understand the reason he wakes you to warn you when evil is present is because he's present and has every intention of protecting you, why do you think he woke up Samuel to let him know that he would become the high priest, he woke up Joseph so that he would get Mary and Jesus to a safe place so what I'm telling you is that if God is waking you up at a usual time instead of becoming fearful become grateful because he's either telling you that he going to protect you from something or he's getting ready to elevate you so start praying and start getting prepared.

Scripture Reference

Hebrews 7:25 - He is able to save forever those who draw near to God through Him, since He always lives to make intercession for them. Hebrews 11:6 - Without faith it is impossible to please Him, for he who draws near to God must believe that He is, and that He is a rewarder of those who seek Him.

Learn To Abide
in the Love of God

Yesterday, we asked God to increase our love for Him and for others. Today, we are going to learn how to abide in this increased love.

What does abiding in God mean?

To stay, remain or leave when God tells you to, abiding in the Lord means that we continually receive, believe and trust that Jesus is everything we need. As disciples, our faith will always be put to the test. abiding allows us to live in, or dwell in, in the same way we live in or dwell in our house. It is the place we reside. Abiding in love means that we can be found residing in love. In the Gospel of John it shows us so many powerful truths about what abiding in love looks like.

In John 15:7-9

It talks about the power of abiding in God's love. It says when we remain in Him and His Word remains in us, we can ask whatever we wish and it will be given to us. He does this for His glory! He loves to see His children prosper as testaments of His power, grace, and mercy. Now here's the thing that I need you to understand that when we abide in his love we must be in the spirit of God which will tell us what to ask for, see too many of us still thinking that God didn't answer our prayers but that's because we keep praying in the natural and not the spirit, see when we pray in the natural we are simply asking God to do it our way but when we pray in the spirit what we ask for will line up with God's plans, God's will and we are able to see our prosperity, our blessing, our healing and our deliverance.

In John 15:26, it speaks on the work of the Holy Spirit. Through our shortcomings and inadequacies, the Holy Spirit testifies of the goodness of God. Through God's completion of us and acceptance of our imperfect selves, we bring glory to Him.

When we abide in His love, the Holy Spirit comes and accompanies us through each phase of our lives on our journey with God.

The love of God operates in us and through us in such a way that the things that used to trip us up, the things that kept us up at night with worry, the obstacles they try and place on your job to keep you from getting paid, or promoted , the foolishness that you sometimes had to go through at home, the things that people do to try and hold us back will not be able to HOLD Us Down, we be like MC Hammer, CAN'T TOUCH THIS!

When we gain the gift of knowing how to abide in God we become more than conqueror we become unconquerable ourselves to any weapon that Satan and his followers try to do. I know firsthand because I have snakes all around me at work and you should see the look on their faces when they start scheming a plan for my bad and God turns it into my God. I know this one is lengthy but it's worth it, I have been dealing with some right out fools on my job and I've been praying and asking God when are they going to realize that they don't know what I know and if they would shut up and ask me how to fix this problem that they have created then things will get better and would you believe the very person that thought they knew more than me that really created the problem came to me in private after he had acted a fool in public and said these exact words you know more about this than I do tell me how are we going fix the problem? Now you tell me what God won't do when you just abide and wait on him.

When we continue to abide in God's word, when we confess with our mouths and believe in our hearts that Jesus Christ is our Lord and Savior SOMETHING is going to happen.

Scripture Reference

John 15:26

But when the Comforter is come, whom I will send unto you from the Father, even the Spirit of truth, which proceedeth from the Father, he shall testify of me:"

_____

_____

_____

_____

_____

52

INCREASING LOVE FOR GOD

I believe our love for God increases the same as any other relationship through growth, trust, dependency and through constant communication and being truthful with ourselves. Our love for God, our love of God fills us with things that the world cannot satisfy us with true dependency, a love that surpasses all love, blessings that no one else can bless us with, a relationship that no one can match, peace that this world cannot give and a love that surpasses all love.

In Luke 10:25-37, Jesus tackles two issues: He not only hangs every commandment and prophecy on two things, you shall love the Lord your God with all your heart, with all your soul, with all your strength, and with all your mind; and your neighbor as yourself, but he also ties love for God and love for people together. Jesus points out to the questioner what the Bible has pointed out to us all along: the more we love God, the more we will love people and the more we will have peace, compassion and understanding. The more we show mercy for people, the more God demonstrates his love and mercy towards us. We cannot be full of the Holy Spirit and fail to walk in love towards people. If we hate people because of their race, their ethnicity, or their financial status or even what they've done to me then God will have no parts of me. The Bible tells us that if we only love those who love us then that is our reward, but we will not have a reward in Heaven. we are a murderer. When we walk in the Spirit of God we must also walk in unconditional love.

Some people do not understand the importance of WORSHIP but there's no worship without love, some people don't understand the importance of assembling and worship together but if we don't have the love of God, our assembling together is in vain.

Now let me state this, I truly believe in order to truly know how to love, we must learn what hate is and how it destroys your life, honestly I don't think I knew what hate was until 2012. Yes that's right don't get me wrong I believe that I had reason earlier or that people did things to me that I thought that I should have hated them for, but in 2012, I went through so much with people that I thought loved me but realized they were the ones that mistreated me. I begin to doubt myself and why I loved anyone or anything, but that was also the year that I started Pastoring at a tiny church. I learned to not only remove hate but I grew in love, I grew in understanding, I grew in grace and I grew in my relationship with God, and he placed me back on my journey to him.

In order for our love for God to increase we have to be open to grow, open to love, open to forgive and most of all available to LOVE.

SCRIPTURE REFERENCE

Luke 10:30-37

And Jesus answering said, A certain man went down from Jerusalem to Jericho, and fell among thieves, which stripped him of his raiment, and wounded him, and departed, leaving him half dead. And by chance there came down a certain priest that way: and when he saw him, he passed by on the other side. And likewise a Levite, when he was at the place, came and looked on him, and passed by on the other side. But a certain Samaritan, as he journeyed, came where he was: and when he saw him, he had compassion on him, and went to him, and bound up his wounds, pouring in oil and wine, and set him on his own beast, and brought him to an inn, and took care of him. And on the morrow when he departed, he took out two pence, and gave them to the host, and said unto him, Take care of him; and whatsoever thou spendest more, when I come again, I will repay thee. Which now of these three, thinkest thou, was neighbour unto him that fell among the thieves? And he said, He that shewed mercy on him. Then said Jesus unto him, Go, and do thou likewise."

1 John 2:15-17

Love not the world, neither the things that are in the world. If any man love the world, the love of the Father is not in him. For all that is in the world, the lust of the flesh, and the lust of the eyes, and the pride of life, is not of the Father, but is of the world. And the world passeth away, and the lust thereof: but he that doeth the will of God abideth for ever.

53

HIS ANGELS SHALL WATCH OVER ME

Psalms 91:11-12
For He will give His angels charge concerning you, to guard you in all your ways. They will bear you up in their hands, lest you strike your foot against a stone.

Too many of us Christians read past this promise with very little thought about the magnitude of what is really being said here or we don't understand it's importance or power.

Only after we get to Heaven will we realize all the things from which we were spared because of the intervention of God's angels on our behalf. I think it's because we continue to seek God's understanding using earthly knowledge and concepts when we are dealing with a beautiful Spiritual Being.

I am sure you have read many of stories about Angels protecting, guiding or warning bible in the Bible but are you aware that those same Angels are at your doorstep and are there for you as well?

But It is possible "to entertain angels without knowing it" as it says in Hebrews 13:2, but sadly, I believe most Christians tend to disregard the ministry of angels altogether.

When we look to God as the source of our protection and provision, the angels are constantly rendering us aid and taking charge of our affairs. Psalm 103:20 says, "His angels mighty in strength...obey the voice of His Word." As we proclaim God's Word, the angels hasten to carry it out. Faith is what releases this promise to work on our behalf.

Angelic protection is just another one of the unique ways in which God has provided protection. He charged angels to guard us in all our ways.

The two most famous examples of angels in the Bible (and the only ones given names) are the angel Gabriel who stands in the Lord's presence (Luke 1:19), and Michael who fights against Satan and the enemies of God (Revelation 12:7). The angel of the Lord is another prominent angel in the Bible.

Angels are supernatural beings that reside in heaven with God, acting as his servants and messengers. Taking a human form, they act as a point of contact between heaven and the human world.

Let me share this story with you, I have been protected by, spoiled by and saved from danger so many times in my lifetime but I remember this one time that I was going through a lot of foolishness on my job and I realize now that it was always right before God would bless me that I dealt with some foolishness but I was being attacked because I was learning more, and faster than anyone else on the job. It seemed like the more I did to improve things on the job the more I caught hell on the job and I remember getting there really early one day and as I was praying a woman came up to me and asked, "Is this Scholar Craft? She explained that she was sent there the temp company. I gave her directions on where to go, but honestly the whole encounter felt strange. Later that day and the next day I noticed her watching every time I would pass by her, so I thought she liked me. This happened for two days and on the third day as I got to work early again, she was there and she came up to me and just started prophesying on me and told me that God hears my prayers, that it wasn't just one person on that job that feared me but it was several and God would weed them out. She continued to tell me that I would be blessed on that very job, shortly after that the Plant Manager was fired and I became the rest of the supervisor's boss. I got promoted to Assistant Plant Manager and guys I can't make this up, that was the last time I saw this woman and when I asked if she was a prophet, she replied like Jesus, she said some say I am and walked off.

Guys God hasn't left us we have to Holy Spirit to guide us and protect us, and we have Angel that God has placed in places for our protection and warning.

Scripture Reference

Psalms 9:11-12

For He shall give His angels charge over you, To keep you in all your ways. In their hands they shall bear you up, Lest you dash your foot against a stone.

54

THOUGH A THOUSAND FALL

Psalms 91:7 A thousand may fall at your side and ten thousand at your right hand; but it shall not approach you.

Question do you have the ability and courage to trust God's Word enough to believe that He going to do actual what he said he would do? To the ones that's actually reading these messages I want you to know that God will do exactly what he said he would do but some things are received at the level of your faith.

With God ALL things are possible but with man we continue to seek God from a natural perspective when he is a spiritual being and what we are dealing with is spiritual but we keep trying to fix it using natural man's ability but let me ask you this question? If we truly believe God is capable of doing what he says he will do again why are we dwelling on earthly situations?

In Luke 4:27, "There were many lepers in Israel in the time of Elisha, but none of them was cleansed." Only Naaman, the Syrian, was healed when he obeyed in faith. Not everyone will receive the benefits of this promise in Psalm 91. Only those who believe God and hold fast to His promises will profit; nevertheless, it is available. To the measure we trust Him, we will, in the same measure reap the benefits of that trust.

God knew there would be times when all we would hear from this world would be so many negative reports, see so many needs, and encounter so much danger around us that we would feel overwhelmed. That is why He warned us ahead of time. We have a choice to make. We can either choose to run to Him in shelter of faith, and we will not be overcome or overwhelmed by the things going on around us or we can live our lives in fear, in poverty, no hope and consumed by the things of this world.

So many Believers have become defeated, not because God doesn't provide, shelter and protects us but rather it's because we have allowed Satan to convince us that our lives do not matter and we are stuck forever where we are right now. Some of us because we are trying to over think God. Naaman almost missed his blessings because he thought more of himself than what he was, he has assumptions of what God should do rather than seeking God's plan and he didn't want to OBEY or TRUST the word of God in its entirety!

I just wish that I could have been there with Naaman when he got in the river too deep like most of us I can imagine when he dipped those first couple of times he didn't feel different or could see a change but I'm so glad that he didn't stop. He remained obedient and continue to deep I can just see him around that fourth or fifth time he could feel and see him old self, he could feel his change coming but he didn't stop there he remained faithful and continued to deep all 7 times because he knew what we need to know today that 7 represents

COMPLETION, he didn't just want to be healed on the other side but he wanted his spirit healed, he wanted his heart heal so that he could love God and man.

In Psalm 91 is the preventive measure that God has given to His children against every evil known to mankind. No place else in the Word are all the protection promises (including help from angels, as well as promises ensuring our authority) accumulated in one covenant to offer such a total package for living in this world.

Too many of us still look at God's word as good reading or one of my favorite that I hear often The Bible was written in the Bible days, I want to know what days are you living in because as for me and my house we are living the Bible every single moment, and day of our lives, each day that I wake up I'm thankful and living, loving and trusting the Bible as my guide to find God, Jesus. The Holy Spirit and my complete healing, protection and blessings.

Scripture Reference

2 KINGS 5:9-14

9 So Naaman came with his horses and with his chariot, and stood at the door of the house of Elisha.

10 And Elisha sent a messenger unto him, saying, Go and wash in Jordan seven times, and thy flesh shall come again to thee, and thou shalt be clean.

11 But Naaman was wroth, and went away, and said, Behold, I thought, He will surely come out to me, and stand, and call on the name of the Lord his God, and strike his hand over the place, and recover the leper.

12 Are not Abana and Pharpar, rivers of Damascus, better than all the waters of Israel? may I not wash in them, and be clean? So he turned and went away in a rage.

13 And his servants came near, and spake unto him, and said, My father, if the prophet had bid thee do some great thing, wouldest thou not have done it? how much rather then, when he saith to thee, Wash, and be clean?

14 Then went he down, and dipped himself seven times in Jordan, according to the saying of the man of God: and his flesh came again like unto the flesh of a little child, and he was clean.

_____

_____

_____

_____

_____

_____

_____

_____

_____

_____

_____

About the Author

Vince Earl Jackson, a man of unwavering dedication and service, was born in Kimberly, Alabama to Willie Bailey and Eunice Jackson. Growing up in a large family of five brothers and five sisters, Vince learned the values of hard work, perseverance, and the importance of family bonds from an early age.

After graduating from Faulkner University with a Bachelor of Science Degree in Management of Human Resources, Vince embarked on a remarkable journey of service to his country. He answered the call to duty and served in the United States Army, Army National Guard, and the Army Reserves for an impressive 29 years. Throughout his military career, Vince exemplified courage, leadership, and selflessness, earning the respect and admiration of his fellow soldiers and superiors alike. His commitment to excellence and his dedication to the well-being of his comrades-in-arms earned him several prestigious awards.

Beyond his military service, Vince is a loving husband to his beloved wife Sabrina Jackson, and together they have raised five wonderful children: Valencia, Karlos, Oliver, Saniya, and Vince. His devotion to his family knows no bounds, and he takes immense pride in being a dedicated husband, father, and grandfather. With two beautiful granddaughters and a handsome grandson, Vince cherishes every moment spent with his growing family, passing down the values of love, integrity, and faith.

In addition to his roles within his family and the military, Vince is also a respected plant manager at a prominent manufacturing company. His leadership skills, honed through years of military service and academic training, have made him an invaluable asset to his company, where he oversees operations with efficiency and expertise.

Despite his many achievements and responsibilities, Vince remains grounded in his faith and his commitment to serving others. He finds joy and fulfillment in being a devoted child of God, actively involved in his community as a mentor, coach, and role model. Vince strives to live out his faith and values each day, aspiring to be the person that God ordained him to be.

In all aspects of his life, Vince Earl Jackson embodies the virtues of service, integrity, and love. His legacy of dedication and leadership will continue to inspire those around him for generations to come, leaving a mark on the hearts and minds of all who have the privilege of knowing him.

References

King James Version of The Holy Bible

New Living Translation of The Holy Bible

Websters Dictionary